A Writer's Guide

handbook for the writer's craft

by *Margaret Blanchard*

with drawings by S.B. Sowbel

Based on *The Writer's Workshop*
by Margaret Blanchard and Cornelius Novelli

Based on The Writer's Workshop
by Margaret Blanchard and Cornelius Novelli (Syracuse, 1966)

ISBN-13: 978-1532841415
ISBN-10: 1532841418

book design & layout by Dana Dwinell-Yardley

contents

one

the act of writing

William Carlos Williams, poet and doctor, writes, *"When I cannot write, I'm a sick man and want to die. The cause,"* he says, *"is plain."*

Why do those of us who write feel this way about the process? Although the cause is plain to Dr. Williams, it may not be obvious to someone who chooses another way of expressing self, recording experience, processing, relating, meditating, discovering.

Whatever our own personal motivations, writing is for many of us a way of self-healing, self-discovery, a path to understanding and empathizing with others and, perhaps if we're lucky, a mode of communication with a more expansive reality than the one we encounter on a daily basis.

For that reason many more of us than ever admit it are writers, scribbling our responses to life in notebooks, journals, or on the back of envelopes. And even more of us are composers of words, dialogues, scenes, memories, fantasies, calling to mind worlds upon worlds of experience and reflection that somehow never actually get written down.

A writer knows how transforming an experience it is, in itself, to actually write something down, whether or not anybody else reads it. That which you wrote speaks back to you over a period of time, changing you as you change it, while both affect the changing reality reflected in the writing. Writing which is shared with others has an even greater reverberation and transforming power. We discover in the process how much we are who we describe ourselves to be and the extent to which our self-awareness conditions what we do and how we do it.

Because of this power, writing involves a commitment, whether what you write is buried in a drawer or published nationally. This commitment has a double edge. On the one hand, it creates a tangible reality which can make things happen. On the other hand, the task of actually recording experience so that it is truthful, balanced and meaningful is extremely difficult. The hurdles to successful communication are many: the language itself, which can never fully describe an experience; the social climate it is spoken within; one's own biased or limited perspective; the so-called value or interest of one's experience; one's own laziness or lack of discipline; and the stereotypes, taboos, and other restrictions on expression imposed by others.

These hurdles can serve as obstacles or challenges:

> *Writers speak of the necessity of writing…as a spiritual compulsion, a straining of the mind to attain heights surrounded by abysses and…at the moment when art attains its highest attainment it reaches beyond its medium or words or paints or music, and the artist finds himself realizing that these instruments are inadequate to the spirit of what he is trying to say.*
>
> —Stephen Spender

> *The voice of despair arrives as a kind of terror…I am certain before I begin writing a piece that I will not be able to put sentences together, or worse, that all I have to say has been said before, that there is no purpose, that there is not intrinsic authority to my own words. And that is where the struggle begins. Because I must then find the place in myself where my words have authority, some true and untouched place that does not matter what has been said before, that speaks feelingly, enough to electrify the rhythms of speech, and make in the very telling a proof of authenticity.*
>
> —Susan Griffin

Other writers, however, find the process exhilarating, or fun:

> *Sitting at my desk one morning, I "pushed off" and with a tingle of not altogether pleasurable excitement and alarm, felt myself "going." I "went" almost as precipitately as skis go down a long white slope, scribbling as rapidly as my pencil could go, indicating whole words with a dash and a jingle, filling page after page with scrawls.*
>
> —Dorothy Canfield Fisher

> *I have always found writing pleasant, and don't understand what people mean by the "throes of creation."*
>
> —E.M. Forster

In any case, for many of us, as for William Carlos Williams, some form of self-expression and creative activity is necessary to our own personal survival, health, and growth. So despite the obstacles and distractions, we keep on writing.

Compared to other means of self-expression, writing has certain advantages. It costs no more to do than the price of pencil and paper; the actual writing down process takes as much or as little time as one has; and the final product doesn't take up much space. The concentration and reflection we develop as writers is socially useful, whether or not we ever publish—and the process of writing brings clarity, creativity and the joy of discovery into our lives.

Like other creative activity, the act of writing is, primarily, intensely individual—although because of the nature of language, it is paradoxically a peculiarly social action as well. Even when it does not focus directly upon one's own self or experience, it is shaped out of one's own responses to the world; the writer alone can do the shaping. The act of writing is also a complex mingling of play and hard work, self-fulfillment and self-effacement.

Pains must be taken so that words will not stand as a barrier but as a medium for experience. Almost by definition a writer is one who has learned to rewrite...and rewrite. Although the best writing usually seems to have been written effortlessly, the effort involved can be tremendous, as Yeats points out in "Adam's Curse":

> *A line will take us hours maybe;*
>
> *Yet if it does not seem a moment's thought,*
>
> *Our stitching and unstitching has been naught.*

Because this translation of experience into sounds, words, rhythms and structures requires concentration, we suggest that the writer find some private space—"a room of one's own"— in which to write, meditate, create.

Words, like physical objects, have weight, shading, resonance, transparence, momentum. The handling of words, with all their possibility of human meanings, is a basic skill the writer develops constantly. Underlying this growth of craft, and just as important, is the growth of consciousness. The writer's continual insight into the world and self requires a continued personal extension, imagination, expansion, a continued effort to perceive and understand, both in solitude and society.

Sometimes you will come to the act of writing with your ideas fully thought through and your material clearly in mind. What gets written then is simply a transcript of something already entire, something already conceived. More often, however, as the words take shape in your mind and on the page, new possibilities begin to suggest themselves—new insights, new relationships, new estimates of the scope of the subject. You begin to consult the inner resources you may not have known you had. Robert Frost speaks of a poem's having some "sense of meaning that once unfolded by surprise as it went."

No matter how much research or thought has preceded the writing, your sharpest alertness to yourself and to the rest of the world may come when, and only then, you try to give form to a sentence, a paragraph, an overall structure. The act of writing itself becomes an exploration of reality. Or, as Gertrude Stein put it, "*You will write if you write without thinking of the result in terms of a result, but think of the writing in terms of discovery, which is to say that creation must take place between the pen and the paper, not before in a thought or afterwards in a recasting.*"

We suggest time spent each day writing. As a skill writing is analogous to other skills like swimming or playing an instrument; practice counts for a lot. Don't wait for inspiration; don't expect perfection. Almost all good writing comes through trial and revision—so even though you reject the first sentences you force yourself to write, they are not wasted. They are a first step.

If you experience what is called "writer's block," this attitude helps: at desperate moments when you just cannot write, you might also try saying something as *badly* as you can—pompously, wordily, foolishly, tritely, ignorantly. Then maybe your normal critical faculties, in revulsion, will lead you toward better and better versions. If that doesn't work, simply silence that too harsh judge in your head and get something down on paper. After all, what have you got to lose?

Still, hard as we may eventually work over a piece of paper, many of our best ideas come unbidden from our unconscious, or somewhere else, and we can't force these revelations. Often after we have worked (or only worried) and then had a good night's sleep, or turned our attention to something else, the solution comes with surprising ease.

> Anyhow this records the odd horrid unexpected way in which these things suddenly create themselves—one thing on top of another in about an hour. So I made up Jacob's Room *looking at the fire…; so I made up* The Lighthouse *one afternoon in the Square here.*
>
> —Virginia Woolf

Relaxing or absorbing activities, often solitary ones, like sports, walking, driving, routine but not exhausting physical work, give the subconscious a chance to integrate the material in a new way. The pattern is to engage the conscious part of the mind actively with the problem, then allow the unconscious, if it will, to re-organize the problem in its own terms. While you cannot count on the effect, you can create the conditions.

> I do believe the writer should know all he can. No subject is alien to him, and the profounder his knowledge in any direction, the more

depth there will be to his writing. I believe that he should be thoroughly grounded in both the old and the new forms, but I am firmly convinced that he must never respect tradition above his intuitive self. Let him be sure of his own sincerity above all, let him bow to no public acclaim, however alluring, and then let him write with all courage what his subconscious mind suggests to him.

—Amy Lowell

two

the seed of the experience

*J*ust as what we experience is only a glimpse of the whole, so what we record of experience is also of necessity partial. One can write, and some have written, volumes describing one event, one moment and still not reach the limits of it. Writing can never present the whole of consciousness; nor can most consciousness register the whole of experience.

Yet there is rarely an occurrence in our lives, however seemingly trivial, that does not yield a single insight for us to take along to share with someone else. Just as we pick up a tiny shell to remind us of a certain day at the beach, so as writers we record a certain experience because it was so full of feeling, was particularly sensational, taught us something, gave us insight. Any event which sparks our mind, our feelings, our senses, our imagination is grist for our mill.

Choosing the shell, or in this case, the central truth, impression, feeling or image, can be a painstaking process, but fortunately it often comes like a gift, a flash of inspiration, what James Joyce calls an "epiphany." As Amy Lowell describes it,

> *A common phrase among poets is, "It came to me." So hackneyed has this become that one learns to suppress the expression with care, but really it is the best description I know of the conscious arrival of a poem.*

This seed of an idea, a sensation, an emotion, or a connection is born of the encounter between ourselves and our world (nature, spirit, society, other people, animals, our own shadows and masks). If cultivated with respect and affection, it will serve as the unifying light of whatever we record, holding together and making whole—the magic ingredient of any creative activity—whatever we have chosen to focus on, whatever trail to follow.

The Four Paths

Just as the gardener finds it helpful to know what kind of seed s/he is planting, so too does, the writer find it helpful to know what kind of "seed" s/he's been given so s/he'll know how best to cultivate it. The four most commonly used seeds, or modes of perception, a writer uses are thinking, sensation, emotion, and intuition (a distinction first made by Carl Jung). The heart feels, the mind thinks, the senses perceive, and the imagination makes connections. Each of these modes follows its own rhythm, organization, and ultimate structure.

For example, we may describe a baseball game according to the physical sensations of a player in the midst of it, or by way of the collective strategy that's supposed to make it work, or through the drama enacted between the catcher and his wife, or from the angle of the fans and what this game symbolizes for them. Each focus follows a different mode of perception, functions differently, and requires a different structuring.

It is important for clarity and integrity to understand how each of these processes works, so we can work with it instead of against it. The heart can and does use the mind to explain itself, but woe unto the heart that lets the mind speak for it. As any lover knows, the senses cannot provide what intuition supplies, nor can imagination substitute for sensation.

If your seed is an idea, then the structure will generally follow a THINK-ING mode, which makes generalizations, and distinctions, defines, classifies, deduces, analyses, traces cause and effect, and often presents information, documentation, opinion, fact, conjecture in a logical, discursive manner. It works most convincingly if one develops a thesis statement and outline. It is useful for arguing for the acceptance of an idea, or for explaining a rational process. For example:

> *Philosophy is a fabric of ideas. It is not, like science, a body of general propositions expressing discovered facts, nor is it a collection of "moral truths" learned by some other means than factual discovery. Philosophy is a stocktaking of the ideas in terms of which one expresses facts and laws, beliefs and maxims and hypotheses—in short, it is the study of the conceptual framework in which all our propositions, true or false, are made. It deals primarily with meanings—with the sense of what we say. If the terms of our discourse are incompatible or confused, the whole intellectual venture to which they belong is invalid; then our alleged beliefs are not false, but spurious.*
>
> —Suzanne K. Langer, *Feeling and Form*

If your seed is a feeling, then the structure will probably follow an **EMOTIONAL** mode, which probes emotions, moods, conflicts, tells stories, weaves descriptions through the interpersonal realms of encounter and response, action and reflection, drama and politics. This works most convincingly if one can focus the predominant feeling clearly and show the underlying conflict or pattern sharply. This is useful for establishing empathy between character and audience, and for presenting an emotion or conflict. For example:

> *I have heard that you intend to settle us on a reservation near the mountains. I don't want to settle. I love to roam over the prairies. There I feel free and happy, but when we settle down we grow pale and die. I have laid aside my lance, bow and shield. I have told you the truth. I have no little lies hid about me, but I don't know how it is with the commissioners. Are they as clear as I am? A long time ago this land belonged to our fathers; but when I go up to the river I see camps of soldiers on its banks. These soldiers cut down my timber; they kill my buffalo; and when I see that, my heart feels like bursting; I feel sorry...Has the white man become a child that he should recklessly kill and not eat? When the red men slay game, they do so that they may live and not starve.*
>
> —Satanta, Chief of the Kiowas,
> from Dee Brown's *Bury My Heart at Wounded Knee*

If your seed is a sensation, then the structure may follow a **SENSITIVE** mode, which explores physical states, feelings, sensory impressions, biological processes, areas of nature, science, energy systems, continuums, and other realms of discovery, experimentation, health and survival. This works most convincingly if one can describe a state or process fully enough for the hearer to experience it. This is useful for sharing a fresh impression or for demonstrating an unusual process. For example:

> *He might have been wind stirring in the valley for all she heard. The fingers of her left hand moved quickly over the cut skin, feeling, pulling the skin apart, holding it, thumb on one side, finger on the other, shaping a red bowed mouth grinning up from the child's neck. "Please!" the man was begging, his voice choked as if from nausea.*
>
> *The knife moved again, and in the silence there came a little hissing. A red filmed bubble streaked with pus grew on the red dripping wound, rose higher, burst; the child struggled, gave a hoarse, inhuman whistling cry. The woman wiped the knife blade on her shoe top with one hand while with the other she lifted the child's neck higher, and then swiftly, using only the one hand, closed the knife, dropped it into her pocket, and drew out a clean folded handkerchief.*
>
> *She gently but quickly wiped the blood and pus from the gaping hole, whispering to the child as it struggled, giving its little hoarse, inhuman cries. "Save yer breath, honey; thet little ole cut ain't nothen for a big boy like you nigh four years old." She spoke in a low jerky voice like one who has run a long way or lifted a heavy weight and has no breath to speak.*
>
> —Harriette Arnow, *The Dollmaker*

If your seed is a connection, then the structure usually follows an **INTUITIVE** mode, which connects disparate parts into one whole which apparently did not exist before the connection was made. While the thinking mode draws lines between entities, the intuitive mode, working with synthesis, symbol, double exposure, association, image, reflection, figurative language, analogy, expansion and contraction, juxtaposition, dream, memory, collage—makes things one again. Intuition will use any device which helps us tie entities together for one brief moment in order to call forth a third, the synthesizing insight, illumination, or inspiration. This works most convincingly if one can capture the reader's imagination by an exact, appropriate, unifying symbol or image. This is useful for revealing dreams and for nurturing them in others. For example:

> *I am an invisible man. No, I am not a spook like those who haunted Edgar Allan Poe; nor am I one of your Hollywood-movie ectoplasms. I am a man of substance, of flesh and bone, fiber and liquids—and I might even be said to possess a mind. I aminvisible, understand, simply because people refuse to see me.*
>
> *Like the bodiless heads you see sometimes in circus sideshows, it is as though I have been surrounded by mirrors of hard, distorting glass. When they approach me they see only my surroundings, themselves, or figments of their imagination—indeed, everything and anything except me.*
>
> —Ralph Ellison, *Invisible Man*

Any effective piece of writing usually employs all four of these modes, subordinating them to its final purpose, but generally one mode serves as a principle of unity, selection and structure, according to the initial seed given, the nature of the work, and the writer's own personal intention and orientation.

> *I tried…to buy some temporary visa into the world of ideas, to forge for myself a mind that could deal with the abstract. In short I tried to think. I failed. My attention veered inexorably back to the specific, to the tangible, to what was generally considered, by everybody I knew then and for that matter have known since, the peripheral. I would try to contemplate the Hegelian dialectic and would find myself concentrating instead on a flowering pear tree outside my window and the particular way the petals fell on my floor.*
>
> —Joan Didion

Along with these experiential seeds, writers, like squirrels, tend to store away potential projects, like nuts waiting to be consumed. These intentions can be helpful as structural principles to build upon, work around, or grow into. If you've ever thought it might be illuminating, effective or fun to compose a musical, tell stories to children, spin visions of a future society, summarize your travels, tell somebody all about your grandmother, expose evil, encourage reform, advocate justice, inspire change, foment revolution, or convince people of the value and enjoyment of participating in a certain activity like playing sports or music, chances are you already have a potential blueprint.

Now might be a good time to bring this intention out and see if you can give it more substance and if you are willing to follow it through to completion. Although trying to fit too many assignments into this one framework might prove somewhat rigid, you're sure to find some assignments useful for exploring the possibilities of this chosen focus and for presenting your material with interest and variety. What might initially serve as mere scaffolding to give form to your writing could easily turn into a structure complete in itself—like a porch.

However, we need to watch out about holding a too finished product in our heads at this point. Just imagine something we once wanted to build. The danger in aiming too high is that our actual production might be crushed by the weight of our aspirations. But if we just keep a meaningful purpose in mind over a sustained period of time, we might be surprised at the results. Even such momentous events as births take place, thanks to the planting of the seed and the nurturing of the egg, only after nine months of darkness.

But in the final writing, no matter how strong our willpower, how solid our form, how focused our seed, each piece of writing will follow its own particular structural demands, just as each meal we cook is unique, recipe or not. The seed of each experience, and its apparent unfolding— however we try to describe, categorize, relate to, imagine or will it—remains a mystery. We cannot know for sure how one revelation will lead into another. As we discover for ourselves what and who we write about, we are guides on the trail for the first time. So we cannot know until the end of the first draft what we have produced or where we have gone. What may emerge in a polished, faceted gem, clear, unified, smooth, has yet to emerge from this cocoon, this circle of energy, this drop of water, this seed of the work we are in the process of writing.

> *As for my next book, I am going to hold myself from writing until I have it impending in me: grown heavy in my mind like a ripe pear; pendant, gravid, asking to be cut or it will fall.*
>
> —Virginia Woolf

three

the voice of the writer

Before we even start writing, we begin to hear the sound of our own voice. As writers we listen to this voice, accept it, and learn how to vary its tones when necessary. Within that subtle sound, so difficult to translate into writing, is the intersection of all the attitudes, personal and social—inherited, earned, and chosen—one has toward one's self, one's subject, and one's audience. It takes courage to let this voice speak out: making a fool of oneself is just as scary as having nothing to say.

The effectiveness of one's tone depends ultimately on the voice which one's writing projects. To know this voice and to allow it to resound with all its uniqueness is one of the challenges of writing. Not to know it is to risk exposure of whatever in that voice is unowned or inauthentic, however it may be disguised by ridicule, irony, platitude or rhetoric. It reveals self-pity as well as self-righteousness, and can unveil those who take themselves too seriously as well as those who can't take anything seriously. There are no forbidden attitudes, however, as long as a writer is conscious enough to use them as s/he chooses.

> *The greatest challenge in writing, then, in the earlier stages was to strike a balance between candor, honesty, integrity, and truth—terms that are fairly synonymous for crossword puzzlers and thesaurus ramblers but hard to equate as living actions. Speaking one's mind, after all, does not necessarily mean one is in touch with the truth or even with the facts.*
>
> —Toni Cade Bambara

A compelling voice is in touch both with self and with the listener, reaching out to draw the other person into a common world, revealing whatever values it has experienced there, and inviting sharing. Hearing this voice, an audience can sense how close to the subject the writer is, how his or her attitude toward it is important, immediate. If the audience trusts the voice, it will also trust that the writer has the ability to recreate the experience in its humanness. This trust is crucial if real communication is to take place. Consider your response to the following passage:

> *The trouble is all in the knob at the top of our bodies. I'm not against the body or the head either: only the neck, which creates the illusion that they are separate. The language is wrong, it should have different words for them. If the head extended directly into the shoulders like a worm's or a frog's without that constriction, that lie, they wouldn't be able to look down at their bodies and move them around as if they were robots or puppets; they would have to realize that if the head is detached from the body both of them will die.*

> —Margaret Atwood

A convincing voice can sound from any style, formal or informal, intimate or distant, and it does not exclude objectivity or detachment. Such a voice, for instance, emerges from E.M. Forster's *Passage to India*, sharing a relationship, a world, and a complexity of attitudes toward its subject, its audience, itself. In this voice we perceive a respect for its subject which is nevertheless objective; a subtlety which invites the reader's participation, and a humorous, ironic awareness of self.

It is difficult, within the accelerated pace and loneliness of contemporary mass society, to find an authentic voice. Various crises of identity, community, and historical continuity make it hard to find an audience we can recognize quickly and speak to honestly and intelligently. It's easier, sometimes, to retreat into the passive voice, which gives us security, a kind of submitting to the inevitable, without exposing our responsibility or emotion; or into jargon which promises the reassurance of being "in"; or into vituperation which helps us feel good about putting others in their place before they put us in ours. We protect ourselves by qualifying statements into pablum. We protect our subject by packaging it, as if it were just another product.

Often when we are not sure to whom we are speaking, we find it hard to speak at all. We must be confident others will listen to and value what we say—yet we wonder if we offend by assuming too much. Thus the writer strives for that ironic overall complex perspective that sees several sides of an issue at once, then runs into the danger of falling into negation or pure indifference.

The dilemma is as much one of character as of craft. One must be both confident and humble, both tolerant and committed. At base writers must find, as best they can, audiences who will listen to what they have to say from the deepest part of themselves—even if that audience is only one—and accept the fact that they cannot reach all. Perhaps in this way they will discover authentic voices that enable them to reach more.

> *I have written so many words*
>
> *Wanting to live inside you*
>
> *To be of use to you*
>
> *Now I must write for myself, for this blind*
>
> *Woman scratching at the pavement with her wand of thought…*
>
> *I look at the face in the glass and see*
>
> *A halfborn woman.*
>
> —Adrienne Rich

This isn't to say that all writing is autobiographical, that the voice speaking in the writing is always the writer's historical self. It does mean that the person speaking, whether close to the writer or far away, is imagined and allowed to speak with all the honesty and precision a writer can command. This, indirectly, calls forth the deepest part of the writer. We can't separate too sharply who we are from who we express.

The same respect we have for self and for characters will flow out to our audience. An audience that is being patronized or flattered can't be fooled for long. There is a delicate but decisive difference between being aware of one's audience and pandering to it. Writers willing to sacrifice the integrity of their communication will offer, or try to sell, only what they think their customers will find acceptable. This is how so many writers for the mass media sink beneath the audience they are talking down to. Creative writers, even when their channels are limited by monetary concerns, will give their best, will respect the needs of their audience, will try to understand, reach out, and open a new world between them.

Ultimately writers need to reconnect with a natural audience of which they are also members. When we feel at home in a shared world, we can speak for people and with them -as well as at them. In such a community one becomes free of that alienation which drives writers and artists to such extremes just to get attention.

The effectiveness of tone also depends on craft—how well one can reproduce what is heard verbally. When we translate spoken language into written symbols, we often find something vital gets left out. Compare a spoken interaction with a written one. Writers struggle to restore the energy of the spoken word, but the process is delicate and often enough, despite skillful handling of materials, they end up with only a crude approximation of what they wanted to say. The tones possible to a person speaking are flexible, multi-hued, but when we try to create them in blocks of written words (even words meant eventually to be spoken, as with a play script), the essence frequently eludes us.

Take, for example, the difference between a letter written by a stranger and one by a close friend. In the latter we can hear a familiar voice. The stranger's may be a puzzle. Did she mean what she said? Is he joking? Is this a compliment or an evasion? But the friend's letter, despite all the potential confusions from unreadable handwriting to disagreements, can be heard. Behind her words we hear the echo of her real voice and through its intonations, we know what she means.

Writing, by its nature, is one step removed from direct communication which is usually achieved through sound, gesture and speech. But writers have also the advantage of this distance. If there are times when they must settle for less than what a live speaker could say, there are other times when they can contrive to say more, sometimes with even more power and interest than a speaker. Like the writer, the speaker may have conflicting attitudes, a confusion at any given moment about what she means, an inability to say what she intends, an uncertainty about her audience and her place in it, and about whether she can do more than just impress, defend or entertain—but unlike the writer, the speaker does not actually see what she is saying. Where the speaker may not be able to get free of this confusion, the writer can read and reconsider.

Writers actually have many devices to help them express what the speaker conveys by gesture, inflection, pause and stress. These devices range from simple marks of punctuation, which can become for a writer a whole system of tonal shorthand, to the infinite resources of sentence variety and overall structure. Note, for example, the variety of effects achieved by Salinger through repetition, dashes, italics, word choice:

> *Do you want to hear something funny? Something really funny? In almost four years of college—and this is the absolute truth—the only time I can ever remember even hearing the expression "wise man" being used was in my freshman year, in Political Science. And you know how it was used? It was used in reference to some nice old poopy elder statesman who'd made a fortune in the stock market.*

Vocabulary is another important tonal device. The level of diction used can reveal a great deal about the speaker's relation to his audience, his ease with his subject, and his confidence in his values. The startling or vivid word can command its own emphasis. The common word can establish its own intimacy.

> *My education and that of my Black associates were quite different from the education of our white schoolmates. In the classroom we all learned past participles but in the streets and in our homes the Blacks learned to drop S's from plurals and suffixes from past tense verbs. We were alert to the gap separating the written word from the colloquial. We*

learned to slide out of one language and into another without being conscious of the effort. At school, in a given situation, we might respond with "That's not unusual." But in the street, meeting the same situation, we easily said, "It be's like that sometimes."

—James Baldwin

A truly effective tone depends finally on our ability to expand to embrace a larger audience. Our language, because of our history as a melting pot, affords a great variety of options when it comes to choosing words, levels of diction, degrees of formality and intimacy, styles and rhythms. We have a richness of sounds, strains, dialects and melodies in our pluralism to draw upon if we allow ourselves access. To be able to do this, we need, without losing connection with our roots, to discuss our lives and issues with wider spectrums of people. Without losing respect for the way we truly speak, if we can break out of habitual language patterns—expressive and comfortable though they feel most of the time—and learn other dialects, we can extend the range of our own voice.

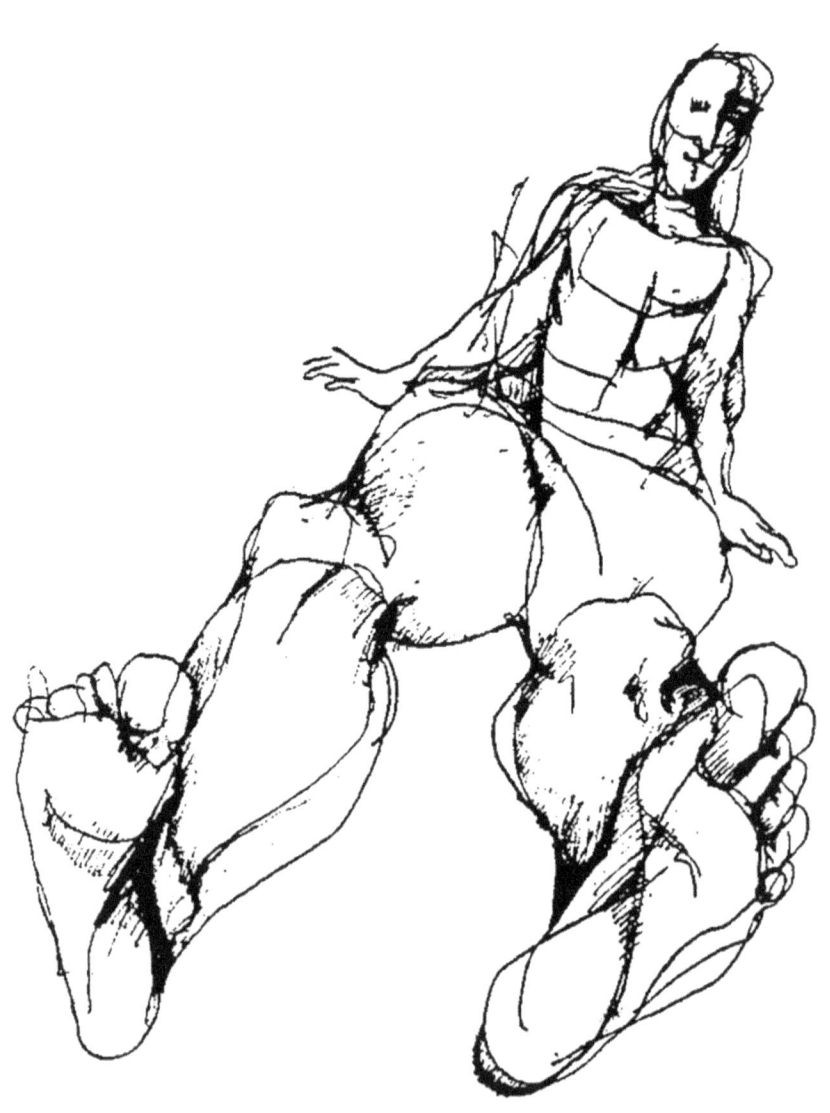

four
the writer's perspective

While writers' own voices are the deepest integration of all the voices they have ever heard—honed down to their own unique sound—so a writer's perspective is a synthesis of all s/he has seen—focused down to one unique viewpoint. The combination, skillfully handled, weaves a rich tapestry of revelation.

There are two important aspects of perspective writers must be conscious of: one, the habitual way they view life, the frame; the other, the specific point of view they choose to show a particular experience, the focus.

The Frame

The habitual furniture of our consciousness is usually either inherited—class attitudes, racial secrets, ethnic jokes—or acquired—political affiliation, religious practice, artistic pursuits. Many of these stances or roles, while comfortable, are fairly predictable. If familiar to the audience, they can be communicated by a kind of shorthand of labels or gestures, or, if not familiar to the audience, by a description of the material conditions from which they emerged.

Because our perspectives are usually shared with a large number of other people, how we frame our own outlook can be tricky. If it's too familiar to our audience, they might nod, stirring only at those points where we fail to toe the line. If it's not familiar enough, they might feel left out and begin to stereotype: "Oh yeah, just another Irish Catholic working class poet babbling away over his brew." Either way we risk losing reader interest and ability to hear what we have to say.

Writers need to detach themselves somewhat from their worlds to be able to see them freshly, clearly. Without viewing them completely through somebody else's eyes—which could be a cop-out—they need to understand how a stranger entering this world might see it. Rather than overstuffing their prose with detailed descriptions of well-worn viewpoints which sit there unmoving like sofas, they need to be able to step back and view the whole, seeing the contradictions between pieces, as well as the underlying patterns.

Readers may already know there's nothing new under the sun, but still they come to the writer for something fresh and interesting. Although it's very difficult for a writer, or any craftsperson, to fashion an entirely new structure or angle of vision acceptable to the public, neither do people want to be reminded too insistently of time-tested truths. This is a risky venture for any writer. S/he must learn how to give the reader enough familiar rope to hang onto, while as guide s/he leaps onward to reach new ground that everyone can stand on. Writers vary in courage, stride and pace in this regard, and there are no rules. They also serve who only watch and write.

Writers' overall perspectives will affect what they see and how they see it: which details they notice, what kind of people they describe, what conflicts they view as important. A woman who works an elevator from three to eleven in an apartment building is not likely, for instance, to have the same perspective as the lawyer she transports up and down. Where a liberal will call for a cause, a Christian will call for a prayer, a Marxist for justice, a Freudian for dreams, a feminist for choice, a humanist for balance, a comic for laughs, a pessimist for sympathy, and a parliamentarian for order.

Whatever our categories, our outlook is often what gives coherence to what we write. It has no business, usually, being explained, but if it operates without the writer's being aware of it, its effectiveness can be diminished. For that reason it is helpful for writers, in journals or letter, to periodically review their own points of view, sets of attitudes, and value systems. Meditation is one way of doing this; writing things down and reading them over is another.

The Focus

The point of view from which a writer chooses to record an experience has a dramatic reality in itself which goes beyond the writer's habitual (or limited) perspective. This focus, if described convincingly, when shared with another viewer (the reader), can have a transforming effect on both writer's and reader's perceptions. In any case, this focus defines the dimensions of the writer's vision, whether close or wide-ranging, involved or detached, exterior or interior.

There is a series of choices writers must make to arrive at a consistent and appropriate point of view: whether they are inside or outside a character or scene; how close or how far away, in time as well as space; and how wide-ranging, again in space and time, their perspective. These choices fall along continuums between near and far, self and other. The most expansive perspective is called "omniscient" (godlike); the most contracted is called "first person narration." The most inside self is called "stream of consciousness"; the most outside, "objective" (I am a camera).

Usually you can trust that the point of view you instinctively choose is right for your essay or story, but it is sometimes useful—for variety, character study or philosophic intent — to experiment with others as well. These modes of recording point of view can be described by — but are not limited to — a variety of techniques, listed here according to direction:

FROM THE INSIDE (SELF, SPEAKER, CHARACTER) OUT:

1. Stream of consciousness (the it of us): a rendering in words of the non-verbal flow of consciousness (or subconsciousness) "with its perceptions, thoughts, judgments, feelings, associations, and memories presented just as they occur without being tidied into grammatical sentences or given logical and narrative order." (*A Glossary of Literary Terms*, revised by M.H. Abrams, Rinehard and Company, N.Y.)

> *Example:* "*...the apron he gave me was like that something only I only wore it twice better lower this lamp and try again so as I can get up early I'll go to Lambes there beside Findlaters and get them to send us some flowers to put about the place in case he brings him home tomorrow today I man no no Fridays an unlucky day first I want to do the place up someway the dust grows in it I think while I'm asleep...*"
>
> —James Joyce, *Ulysses*

2. Interior monologue (the conscious reflector): a combination of narration and a direct rendering of the introspective process of a character —more conscious and more selective than stream of consciousness, in the third person usually rather than the first. The writer edits to reveal certain themes or obsessions of the character. As with soliloquy, interior monologue is like overhearing a person thinking out loud or talking to self.

> **Example:** "*Did it matter then, she asked herself, walking towards Bond Street, did it matter that she must inevitably cease completely; all this must go on without her; did she resent it; or did it not become consoling to believe that death ended absolutely? but that somehow in the streets of London, on the ebb and flow of things, here, there, she survived...she being part, she was positive, of the trees at home; of the house there, ugly, rambling all to bits and pieces as it was; part of people she had never met; being laid out like a mist between the people she knew best, who lifted her on their branches as she had seen the trees lift the mist, but it spread ever so far, her life, herself.*"
>
> —Virginia Woolf, *Mrs. Dalloway*

3. First person narration (the verbal I): a rendering of a story by a character speaking for her/himself directly to us, the audience, with her/his own speech patterns, inflections, images, tones. S/he may be the protagonist or just an observer, a reliable or an unreliable narrator.

Example: *"Whether I shall turn out to be the hero of my own life or whether that station will be held by anybody else, these pages must show. To begin my life with the beginning of my life, I record that I was born (as I have been informed and believe) on a Friday at twelve o'clock at night. It was remarked that the clock began to strike, and I began to cry, simultaneously."*

—Charles Dickens, *David Copperfield*

4. Dramatic monologue (Me and You-Understood): a single person speaking at a crucial or dramatic moment to one or more people whose responses remain understood (like hearing one end of a phone conversation).

Example: *"I am poor brother Lippo, by your leave! You need not clap your torches to my face. Zooks, what's to blame? You think you see a monk! What, 'tis past midnight, and you go the rounds, And here you catch me at an alley's end, Where sportive ladies leave their doors ajar?"*

—Robert Browning, *Fra Lippo Lippi*

5. Exhortation (the We) : A speaker making an appeal to a group of people to share a point of view. The use of "we" convinces by assuming they already do.

Example: *"Everything now, we must assume, is in our hands; we have no right to assume otherwise. If we—and now I mean the relatively conscious blacks, who must, like lovers, insist on, or create, the consciousness of the others—do not falter in our duty now, we may be able, handful that we are, to end the racial nightmare, and achieve our country and change the history of the world. If we do not now dare everything, the fulfillment from the Bible in song by a slave is upon us: God gave Noah the rainbow sign, No more water / the fire next time."*

—James Baldwin, *The Fire Next Time*

FROM THE OUTSIDE IN:

6. Objective (the it, out there): a description of events and people from the point of view of a camera, without access at all to their interior thoughts, feelings, impressions—limited to what they say, do or look like. Here the narrator shares the limitations of the audience.

> **Example:** *"Mary sat musing on the lamp-flame at the table*
>
> *Waiting for Warren. When she heard his step,*
>
> *She ran on tip-toe down the darkened passage*
>
> *To meet him at the doorway with the news*
>
> *And put him on his guard. 'Silas is back'*
>
> *She pushed him outward with her through the door*
>
> *And shut it after her. "Be kind,' she said.*
>
> *She took the market things from Warren's arms*
>
> *And set them on the porch, then drew him down*
>
> *To sit beside her on the wooden steps."*
>
> —Robert Frost, *The Death of the Hired Man*

7. Limited: "The author narrates the story in the third person but chooses one character as his 'sentient center' whom he follows throughout the action, restricting the reader to the field of vision and range of knowledge of that character alone." (Abrams, *A Glossary of Literary Terms*)

> **Example:** *"Dilsey prepared to make biscuit. As she ground the sifter steadily above the breadboard, she sang, to herself at first, something without particular tune or words, repetitive, mournful and plaintive, austere, as she ground a faint, steady snowing of flour onto the breadboard. The stove had begun to heat the room and to fill it with murmurous minors of the fire, and presently she was singing louder, as if her voice too had been thawed out by the growing warmth, and then Mrs. Compson called her name again from within the house. Dilsey raised her face as if her eyes could and did penetrate the walls and ceil-*

ing and saw the old woman in her quilted dressing gown at the head of the stairs, calling her name with machinelike regularity."

—William Faulkner, *The Sound and the Fury*

8. Dramatic: a critical interaction between speaker and audience, or between two speakers, with both presented in the third person, but allowed to speak and act for themselves, with little description, no commentary.

> **Example:** *"Goldberg: Well? (McCann does not answer.) McCann, I asked you well.*
>
> *McCann (without turning): Well what?*
>
> *Goldberg: What's what? (McCann does not answer). What is what?*
>
> *McCann (turning to look at Goldberg, grimly): I'm not not going up there again.*
>
> *Goldberg: Why not?*
>
> *McCann: I'm not going up there again."*
>
> —Harold Pinter, *The Birthday Party*

9. Omniscient: "The author tells the story omnisciently, moving from character to character and event to event, having free access to the motivations, thoughts and feelings of his characters and introducing information when and where he chooses." (*A Glossary of Literary Terms*) This point of view gives the clearest sense of the creator at work in her/his own world.

> **Example:** *"And so they remained for many minutes, opposite each other, far apart in silence; Will's face still possessed by a mute rage, and Rosamund's by a mute misery. The poor thing had no force to fling out any passion in return; the terrible collapse of the illusion towards which all her hope had been strained was a stroke which had too thoroughly shaken her: her little world was in ruins, and she felt herself tottering in the midst as a lonely bewildered consciousness ... Will wished that she would speak and bring some mitigating shadow across his own cruel*

speech, which seemed to stand staring at them both in mockery of any attempt at revived fellowship. But she said nothing, and at last with a desperate effort over himself, he asked, 'Shall I come in and see Lydgate this evening?'"

—George Elliot, *Middlemarch*

The techniques writers choose to present their point of view will depend on several factors: the degree of consciousness they wish to convey in their protagonist or narrator; the degree of intimacy between speaker and audience; the angle of involvement between characters and audience; and the ultimate purpose of the piece.

A narrator, by the way, is another potential character, who can also serve either as mask or foil for one's own persona. Although s/he may be a stiff presence to hide behind, s/he can also be designed like a musical instrument to amplify your voice. Perhaps like a child s/he may dare speak out sooner than you.

The purpose of your writing will also help determine the particular perspective you choose. If your interest is scientific description, you might tend toward the objective; if your interest is psychology, you might lean toward the dramatic; if your interest is philosophy, you might drift toward omniscience; and if your interest is mystery, you might master the limited. Much modern fiction, for instance, relies heavily on the limited perspective of the unreliable narrator.

There are no formulas, but there are some rules. The type of narration you are using can be signaled by the pronouns you use—first person, third person, "you", "we". Awareness of shifts, and consistency in pronoun reference help the writer keep the focus clear for the reader.

As point of view locates us in conscious space, so a writer must also pay attention to conscious time, which manifests itself in the tense of verbs: past, present, future, ongoing, perpetual, and so on. Are the events happening in the moment, or are they recollected in tranquility? Are the speakers looking back on their own lives and seeing events as they happened? Although it is acceptable to shift from one tense to another, it is key that you signal each shift to your passengers (the readers), so they don't get jolted or lost; and it goes more smoothly if you remain consistent within each gear. A virtuoso writer can shift back and forth harmoniously, but the beginning writer is not encouraged to overdo such feats.

Ultimately we choose the tense and time frame that will contribute to the pace we need to tell our story. A focused time scheme can also help establish the writer's (and to some extent, the reader's) distance, consciousness, and involvement with the subject. The present tense is usually faster, obviously more immediate, than either past (reflective) or future (visionary). As we choose the pace at which our story unfolds, so too can we choose times and places to reveal its message. Lessons learned "too late" may give fuller truth when recorded in the past tense, whereas a more bitterly felt experience might best be recaptured in the present tense.

These techniques, like any instrument of vision, from telescope to television, are limited to the uses made of them. If handled honestly and deeply, however, they can teach us how to see more compassionately and clearly, without blinders or tinted glasses. This is bound in time to have an enlightening effect on our whole perspective.

five
the lives of characters

The process of characterization can be one of the most enjoyable and rewarding aspects of writing. From simple sketches to complex portraits, characterization yields insights into self, into others, and into the spaces in between. There are three stages to the process of characterization, depending, on the degree to which writers are separate from the character they're describing or presenting.

The first stage is a projection of some aspect of one's self outward. It can be compared to going to a costume party. Writers put on certain masks or play certain roles to highlight one of the many personalities or facets within themselves. Even the writer whose purpose is not characterization engages in this kind of projection through the narrative technique and tone. By focusing through a particular spokesperson or narrative self, by adopting a mask suitable to the subject, each writer personifies to some extent, if for no other sake than reader or "human" interest.

Taking several steps further, writers can manufacture characters by projecting some more private, hidden selves—a shadow, an alter ego, a mirror image, an ideal—onto the stage of their writing. In this phase of characterization the character is still clearly an aspect of the writer, even when referred to objectively as an *other* ("she" or "he"). This phase is useful for presenting types who can serve to illustrate the writer's points, whether political, philosophical, or psychological—but if these characters merely serve these ideas, they remain in a sense puppets. To maintain reader belief, writers must take care to disguise their manipulation of them, and to allow them as much solidity and vitality as possible.

The second stage of characterization is the creation of autonomous persons who have their own integrity, dynamics, and worlds, apart from the writer's. This stage can be compared to giving birth and/or raising children. Although they may emerge from the writer's own imagination and self-awareness, although they may be clearly his/her own objectified self, the purpose here is to allow the characters as much freedom and mystery as fully developed humans have. As any parent knows, this is not easy. The temptation to oversimplify, stereotype, manipulate, and judge—in order to maintain some control over the character—is overwhelming.

To assist the writer in this process of creation and detachment, certain techniques are available. One is dramatization—which presents what a person says and does, the actions which make her/his life significant. By showing rather than telling the reader who the character is, the writer subtly respects both character and reader— by letting characters reveal themselves, and by letting readers understand on their own.

Another method for giving the character autonomy is to show her/him interacting with other characters and to allow them to define one another by responses and by direct descriptions. Their estimates of each other are less likely than an author's comment to be taken as absolute. This method also serves to reveal both characters at once.

A final method for allowing characters to be their own selves is showing them in context: existing in worlds which form their identities and which, in turn, they help to form. Even characters of seemingly independent strength and interest like Falstaff in *Henry IV, 1* or Levin in *Anna Karenina* draw their vitality and profundity from the fictional whole of which they are a part. Surely we cannot understand a character like Holden Caulfield if we do not see him in his fictional world. Presentation of context can also serve as a symbolic mode of character revelation. In *Death of the Heart* Elizabeth Bowen shows persons by showing us their rooms, the worlds they have arranged for themselves, in which they feel most able to cope.

A writer's, like a parent's, freedom and maturity lie in allowing characters to speak for themselves and to act consistently from their own traits. Empathy helps. And so does a respect for the ultimate inviolability of a person. Chaucer, while giving many significant marks and actions—we *know* his characters—never presumes to invade the full innerness of the person. Virginia Woolf deliberately blurs her presentations of personality so that no one will assume that she thinks she can explain all. The reader is left with a sense of the mystery (not to be confused with a failure in clarity), a sense of the dimensions which can be lived in but not spelled out. The secret of free personality eludes one like the whale, which Ishmael *comprehends* in all its irrationality, but never manages to *measure*.

As a writer, then, you need a high degree of tolerance if you are to let character emerge in its own truth, not prejudiced by your own defenses and needs. The underlying approach is to care very much about the character's existence as a human being. This is not necessarily the same as liking him; no one likes Goneril, Regan, Iago, but Shakespeare nevertheless imagined them into intense existence. (You do, however, have to decide if the character is likeable, at least to the other characters; or if they don't know whether or not to like him, this tension will probably become, like paradox within character, a hinging point.)

> *It just seems to me that even the most ordinary person, in real life, will turn out to have something.*
>
> —Anne Tyler

This second stage of character development is useful, essential perhaps, for fiction and drama, where the focus is on the people, what they do, and how they relate.

The third stage of characterization is to establish a connection between an independent person or "character" and the reader. This phase can be compared to matchmaking, or introducing people. The thrust of the characterization is to overcome the gap between two strangers, to make known what is unknown. Here the mystery of the other is already established; a great degree of detachment already exists. Without losing the advantages of this apparent objectivity, the writer must work to bring the character closer to self and to audience. This phase is useful for biography.

While the method of dramatization—showing a character principally through external actions—is also helpful here, the writer at this stage will also rely on description, probing the psyche of the person. Although the challenge in any form of characterization is to reveal the relationship between inner and outer selves, between choices and actions, between feelings and expressions, the writer in this phase is likely to lean more toward analysis and explanation in order to reveal more than may meet the eye of the casual beholder. Here too the writer must resist the temptation to stereotype, to judge, to intrude, to distort. Such egolessness is as difficult to achieve in art as it is in life, but like a good matchmaker, the writer must remain neutral, neither praising nor blaming, leaving it entirely up to readers to decide if they want to "live with" this person or not. To avoid stereotyping it may help to begin thinking about a person where s/he remains a mystery to you, to her/himself, or to some other person in her/his life.

Frequently built into character description is the ambiguity of relationships between appearance and reality: faces, clothing, gestures, environment, social contacts can be both a reflection of deepest selves and masks. But even masks may function differently. Is the mask a disguise, even to the point of being a hypocrisy? Or are there within a person many true selves expressible in various contexts? Huckleberry Finn, for example, wears a variety of masks, with complex minglings of deception and self-expression.

Imagery can often provide suggestive compression in character description. Thus Dylan Thomas' presentation of his uncle as a buffalo and his aunt as a mouse who "whisked about on padded paws, dusting the china dogs, feeding the buffalo, setting the mouse traps that never caught her," keenly describes the couple, and suggests the irony of mouse arguing with buffalo and dominating. This description also presents the writer's own assessment of the relationship with humor and subtlety.

At any stage of characterization, writers must pay special attention to two factors: concretization and selectivity. In these ways, they can retain ultimate control of the process (if not the person), yet must also take responsibility for the final presentation. Even if you choose to analyze a character, you need to show concretely which actions, conflicts, or motives you are focusing on. Readers quickly get bored or suspicious hearing about merely types or thinly veiled projections. Not just satisfied with gossip, most humans are curious to encounter another person in the flesh. Concretization allows readers to enter freely, and at first hand, into the description, and if need be, come to their own conclusions.

While it is true that selectivity makes some distortion inevitable (no biography is ever absolutely true to life), it need not oversimplify or reduce to type. Selection of significant detail heightens certain traits, conflicts, complexities of character to give insight into the most interesting aspects, such as the paradoxes of a person's life, or the multiplicity of facets within one "diamond shape, the single person" (as Virginia Woolf describes Mrs. Dalloway).

Selectivity depends on authors knowing or seeming to know more about characters than they could ever say; and when, from all this, they select the most significant points, they choose those which reflect the complexity of the rest. As a result of this heightened insight, readers often come to think of characters as more real than people they know. Not only do they understand the characters more fully, but they have the sense that there is more *to* understand, more that would be intelligible and interesting.

In non-fiction, apart from biography or profile, there is usually less room for character development *per se*. All the more challenge, then, to a writer's ability to select the telling detail. Writers might study the techniques of portrait artists and photographers who, by catching a fleeting gesture or expression, suggest the full existence of their subjects: What does the subject do with his hands as he talks? What facial expression is most characteristic?

Letting characters speak for themselves: The proverb has it that actions speak louder than words. This is certainly the case where people's actions contradict their speech. But suppose that we think of speech itself *as* an action. Like other actions, it will spring from character. Like other actions, it will be part of a concrete situation, an event in itself, a way for the character to respond to the situation. This means that instead of merely illustrating character, dialogue becomes part of the narrative flow. Talk is not merely talk, but the very substance of what is happening.

It is desirable, though not always possible, for a character's spoken words to be so much a part of her/him that no other character could have said them. Ideally, then, no dialogue would need identifying tags such as "Marvin said." In the interest of narrative power and economy, practice using as few such tags as possible. Learning to do without them will help you to shape dialogue that is more natural and more expressive of character, and you will free your writing from the impediment of unneeded words.

Where you do need dialogue tags, do not be afraid to repeat the simple word "said." A string of variations—*exclaimed, muttered, breathed, intoned, queried, answered*—will be distracting. Better to save such words for the times they are really needed. As a general rule, too, be sparing with adverbs in your dialogue tags, e.g., *he said quietly* (or *abruptly or thoughtfully or coldly*, or...) Apart from avoiding overtones of the Tom Swift school, you should try to get the expressive quality into the speech itself.

One technical point: on the printed page dialogue is more convincing if it consists of brief exchanges, each character speaking relatively few words. No absolute norm can be set, but read the dialogue of various authors and count the number of words in some typical speeches. In non-fiction, direct quotations tend to be longer. Exact reporting, of course, might demand the inclusion of a long quote. But try to break even such necessarily long passages up into natural portions.

Long or short, dialogue should be natural as speech. We have all read dialogue that didn't have the ring of reality. Some writers have a better ear for speech than others, but anyone can cultivate this talent. Saying your written dialogue aloud is a good test to distinguish the natural from the unnatural. Above all, *listen* to the way people sound when they talk.

Oddly enough, if you tape record spontaneous speech and then transcribe the tape into print, the speech often does not seem easy, connected or perhaps even natural. Like most effects, natural-sounding dialogue is achieved by selection.

Dialects are usually thought of as ethnic or regional, e.g. Polish, Southern. But there are others as well. The old, for instance, often speak a different dialect from the young. In a strict sense everyone speaks a dialect—even if it is standard mid-American—and feels other modes of speech to be "dialects," more or less strange, unnatural. Project yourself into the speaker's sense of comfort with her/his own way of speaking (assuming that s/he speaks naturally).

In using non-standard dialects avoid distracting phonetic spellings such as *yew* for you. This is not an easy lesson to learn. Best results come with at most a hint of phonetic spelling. Your aim in writing is not to reproduce the dialect accurately (one could use the phonetic alphabet for that), but to create the illusion of a person speaking. The characters and situation come first.

six

discovery through images

The two dimensions of imagery a writer needs to be conscious of are: the tangible—any concrete appeal to the senses—and the symbolic—any image which is expansive in meaning. The second dimension, although it goes beyond the tangible, remains dependent on it just as the imagination depends for nourishment on physical embodiment. The relation between them, therefore, is never an either/ or choice, since both dimensions inhere in the existence of any image. Even such objective descriptions as the following draw on the expansive, either implicitly or explicitly:

> *so much depends / upon / a red wheel / barrow / glazed with rain / water / beside the white / chickens*
>
> —W. C. Williams

> *Used to just the bare essentials [the cactus] stood on our kitchen windowsill two floors above the inhospitable soil and neither flourished, grew nor died.*
>
> —Irena Klepfisz

> *Her skin had a pattern all its own of numberless branching wrinkles and as though a whole little tree stood in the middle of her forehead, but*

a golden color ran underneath, and the two knobs of her cheeks were illuminated by a yellow burning under the dark.

—Eudora Welty

In that instant, in too short a time, one would have thought, even for the bullet to get there, a mysterious, terrible change had come over the elephant. He neither stirred nor fell, but every line of his body had altered. He looked suddenly stricken, shrunken, immensely old, as though the frightful impact of the bullet had paralyzed him without knocking him down.

—George Orwell

Whether both dimensions are brought to full fruition depends on the skill of the writer, the way the image fits into or ties together the rest of the piece, and the reader's perception. Here Anne Morrow Lindbergh provides, through simile, a limited expansion beyond the tangible:

This is a snail shell, round, fully and glossy as a horse chestnut. Comfortable and compact, it sits curled up like a cat in the hollow of my hand.

Important as imagery is in recreating experience for the reader, it is even more important for the writer. At the heart of the creative process is this ability to perceive the significance of an experience in one unifying image. An example is Buddha's classic sermon on the meaning of life. He didn't say a word; he just stood there holding a flower. According to Thomas Aquinas, "the image is a principle of our knowledge. It is that from which our intellectual activity begins, not just as a passing stimulus but as an enduring foundation." Or as Walt Whitman puts it:

There was a child went forth every day / And the first object he looked upon, that object he became, / And that object became part of him.... / The early lilacs became part of this child...

For the writer, therefore, imagery on the tangible level is an important method for recreating an experience. Our minds are lazy. Asked to recall an event, we bring up all the generalities that have been used about *events like that.* A scene that should be unique, sharply defined, becomes a blurred member, a classification. If writers really want to enter their experience—and it does not matter for the moment whether it is a factual or imagined experience—they must work to capture exact and telling *sensory detail,* floods of it, probably much more than they can get into one piece of writing. They must first become reporters, recorders of life. Selection of exact and telling detail is one of a writer's greatest challenges. By recalling us to tangible existence these details help the reader experience or re-experience what a writer is showing.

Even a simple act like approaching a house and ringing its bell is full of potentially meaningful images: What style house? What color? What condition?—lawn?—porch?—clean or not?—furniture?—toys?—any sounds from within?—smells?—what kind of doorbell and does it work?

Writers' images spring from their own aliveness, from an awareness (often subconscious) of the world around them. They cut through the stereotypes that would muffle their sense of living reality. Accomplished writers of both fiction and non-fiction use images along with, or instead of, abstractions because words like *joy, sorrow, noise, fresh* cannot be assumed to mean to one person what they mean to another. The sharpest detail by which Hamlet knows his mother's "frailty" is that she remarried *"ere those shoes were old with which she followed my poor father's body. . .to the grave."*

In using images, it is generally best to let one sense initially dominate:

> *There's the clip clop of horses on the sunhoneyed cobbles of the humming streets, hammering of horseshoes, gobble quack and cackle...*
>
> —Dylan Thomas

> *There was a cold night smell in the chapel. But it was a holy smell. It was not like the smell of the old peasants who knelt in the back of the chapel at Sunday Mass. That was the smell of air and rain and turf and corduroy.*
>
> —James Joyce

When you have a variety of sense impressions, bring them in naturally, as they might occur in an observer's or participant's awareness. Thus in "A Narrow Fellow in the Grass," Emily Dickenson moves from the sight of a snake to the resulting internal sensations, "a tighter breathing, And zero at the bone"—*tighter* suggesting unnatural constriction, *zero*, both a contrasting hollowness and a coldness.

Perhaps the most common sensory perceptions are those that have to do with spatial relationships—location, appearance, mass, motion. Normally the sense of sight is the basis for this kind of ordering, since we perceive most spatial patterns visually. But it is quite possible to create a sense of spatial orientation by appealing to other senses such as hearing and smell.

Remember that although the standard list of five senses is valid—sight, smell, hearing, touch, taste—many additional senses and sub-senses make up the texture of experience: kinesthetic sense (internal sensations of bodily movement, tension, placement); balance; pressure or lack of it inside the body (a cold gives us a "stuffed head"); aridity or wetness, temperature. Such feelings are captured in the following:

> *The heart rears wings bold and bolder / And hurls for him, o half hurls earth for him off under his feet.*
>
> —G.M. Hopkins

> *After great pain a formal feeling comes / The nerves sit ceremoniously like tombs. / The stiff Heart questions… / The feet mechanical / Go round their wooden way… / This is the hour of lead / Remembered if outlived / As freezing persons recollect the snow—/ First chill, then stupor, then the letting go.*
>
> —Emily Dickenson

What is known as symbolic or figurative language (analogy, simile, metaphor) takes this faithful and articulate detail one step further (as do some of the examples above) and connects it to a broader reality, usually through some intuitive leap or expansion that identifies the concrete tangible reality to some emotional, psychic or spiritual reality that is not otherwise tangible, creating what is called the "concrete universal." The writer or artist with this ability can serve as a medium for this creative energy which widens our circles of consciousness and connection.

Although sometimes dismissed as "merely figurative," not real, metaphors and similes are often the only precise way to grasp what is real. One symbolic gesture or detail, like Othello's putting out the light before he murders Desdemona, may carry more meaning than any explanation.

Selection is key to figurative language. Just as you choose one striking sense impression out of a myriad of possibilities, so too you select one of these images as having the potential to unify the whole as a symbol. Such a symbolic pattern can create a structure within itself which, if well highlighted, gives larger significance and mobility to the whole work. In this way imagery serves as a structural principle as well as communication device.

There are many ways of saying one thing and meaning others. The following list of **figurative devices** provides some definitions and examples of the wide variety possible:

INVOLVING A COMPARISON:

Analogy: comparison between the unknown, complex or abstract and the known, simple or concrete for purpose of explanation:

> *It is with words as with sunbeams—the more they are condensed, the deeper they burn.*

Metaphor: implied comparison between things essentially unlike (identification or substitution):

> *In a Station of the Metro— The apparition of these faces in the crowd / Petals on a wet black bough.*

Simile: an expressed comparison (by "like," "as," "than," "similar to"):

And her mouth is sweet as a honey flower cold / But her heart is heavy as bags of gold.

Metonymy: identification of the whole with related or associated image:

The pen is mightier than the sword.

Synecdoche: comparison of part with whole or whole with part:

Hired hand.

Personification (including Apostrophe): comparison between human and other:

Joy and Temperance and Repose / Slam the door on the doctor's nose.

Allusion: comparison of something with historical, literary, mythological persons, places, events, images:

Nature and Nature's laws lay hid in night:

God said, "Let Newton be!" and all was light.

Synaesthesia: comparison between senses:

The trumpet blared red.

I heard a fly buzz when I died... With blue uncertain stumbling buzz.

The morning light creaks down again.

INVOLVING A COMPARISON PLUS:

Symbol: something which means what it is and more than it is (symbols can be open in meaning or closed):

O Rose, thou art sick!/ The invisible worm / That flies in the night, / In the howling storm,/ Has found out thy bed / Of crimson joy, /And his dark secret love Does thy life destroy.

INVOLVING A COMPARISON MINUS:

Allegory: a narrative or description that has a real meaning beneath the merely surface one:

> Dante's *Divine Comedy*; Christ's parables.

INVOLVING A CONTRAST:

Paradox: apparent contradiction which is nevertheless somehow true (can be of statement and of situation):

> *My life closed twice before its close.... Parting is all we know of heaven / And all we need of hell.*

Oxymoron: condensed paradox:

> *Sophomore (wise fool).*

Understatement: saying less than one means:

> *I gave commands; then all smiles stopped together.*

Overstatement: saying more, or exaggerating:

> *All night I made my bed to swim; with my tears I dissolved my couch.*

Irony: a discrepancy between what one says and what one means (verbal); between appearance and reality, or expectation and fulfillment (situational); between what an actor says or does and what the author and audience know (dramatic):

> *I met a traveler from an antique land/ Who said, "Two vast and trunkless legs of stone / Stand in the desert. Near them, on the sand, / Half sunk, a shattered visage lies, whose frown, / And wrinkled lip, and sneer of cold command, / Tell that its sculptor well those passions read /Which yet survive (stamped on those lifeless things) / The hand that mocked them and the heart that fed;/ And on the pedestal these words appear: / My name is Ozymandias, king of kings; / Look on*

my words, ye Mighty and despair!/ Nothing beside remains. Round the decay / Of that colossal wreck, boundless and bare / The lone and level sands stretch far away."

—Shelley

Images do not automatically bring substance and immediacy to writing. Used mechanically they only result in the facile, the obscure, or the trite. Some journalistic styles lean heavily for effect on showy, even virtuoso metaphor making, often with results more dazzling than significant. Be extravagant in your journals and first drafts, especially if images are not easy for you, but in your final draft, the image that strikes you as extraordinarily clever might be one you should remove. "Murder your darlings," as Sir Arthur Quiller-Couch put it.

It takes more than just imagination and wit to create memorable figurative language. It also takes an intuitive power rooted in the common ground of our collective consciousness. No artist or writer, no matter how isolated, can grow or communicate alone.

Developing that deeper intuitive power, and trusting it, is a challenge for all of us in this highly rational, functional society where intuition is often dismissed as childish or womanish. It calls for a different kind of consciousness, a non-judgmental, all-inclusive awareness of process, a spontaneous knowing, an immediate perception of oneness, wholeness, and harmony. It requires a deeper receptivity than is available to the active imagination spinning its wheels on surface connections.

Fortunately recent discoveries of the importance of the "other" side of the brain—the right side, which is non-verbal, imagistic, and intuitive, expressing itself through fantasy, pattern, sound, body language and dreams—have enabled us to reaffirm this part of ourselves. Reclaiming this magical part is proving to be a healing experience for many people, not just writers. While the rational side of the brain makes us aware of the distinctions, discriminations, and schisms between us and the rest of the world, the intuitive side tunes us into widening circles of light, sound, and vibration which encompass us *and* the rest of the world.

What a difference this makes for creative persons. In a rational world they must juggle realities like separate entities which come together only by virtue of magic. Their ability to create the illusion of oneness falls apart as soon as they stop their act. In an intuitive world, suddenly they can draw on a natural fusion which, like the sun which shines on everybody, includes both positive and negative poles. This kind of energy can transform as well as translate one reality into another.

All those devices dismissed by the hitherto dominant rationalists become potent: superimpositions, hindsight, foresights, insights, inner voices, juxtapositions, epiphanies, "willing suspensions of disbelief," guesses, faith, theories, hunches, flashes, leaps, designs, nonsense, and play. No longer do we feel "crazy" when one half of our mind speaks back to the other half. In this freer context both these modes can work together for coordination and synthesis. Writers who can root themselves in both these essential halves of the brain is rich in both resources and skills.

As one grounds oneself in the intuitive process, one discovers two basic laws of intuition, out of which all symbol-making grows: The first is *correspondence* or analogy (Blake's "to see the world in a grain of sand"), which identifies such apparent dualities as microcosm/macrocosm, inside/outside, back/front, light/shadow, expansion/contraction (yin/yang), as if each polarity mirrors the other. The second law is *simultaneity* (or Jung's "synchronicity") or coincidence (Blake's "to see eternity in an hour"), which identifies points on a space/time continuum as one, rather than separated into past, present, and future. This yields such experiences as *déjà vu*, "time released," incremental repetition, reverberation, bleed-through, rhythms and recurring patterns. The first law expresses itself symbolically as a circle, and the second symbolically as a cycle (or spiral).

To train one's intuition it seems essential to draw first on already developed systems of intuitive wholeness. The primary system, from which all others draw, is nature, her cycles of night and day, the seasons, the sun, moon, planets and stars, as well as plants, rocks, rivers, mountains, wind, clouds, ocean and sky. Derived from the rhythms of this fundamental reality are the great intuitive systems which can guide persons in their search for images which are meaningful because they are grounded in human consciousness: the *I Ching*, astrology, the Tarot, Native American medicine wheels and Hindu mandalas, and the mythologies, art and scriptures of the oldest cultures. (Jung's study of the collective unconscious, *Man and His Symbols*, and Campbell's study of the "monomyth" are good starting points.)

Confused by the notion that creativity requires starting from scratch, some modern writers can get lost in the obscurity of isolated imaginings, in the fragmentation of manufactured worlds. To discover the whole worlds contained within us, we often need to tap into some deeper, communal, time-honored sources. Not that any of these systems should be swallowed whole (the other way of losing oneself). By living with them for awhile, however (not just studying but actually incorporating them into one's life), a writer can find tools with which to discover new intuitive territory and create new visions.

Some important intuitive tools are: dreams (the first and most revealing source of images); color and the spectrum or rainbow (both symbol and reality of wholeness); drawing, which taps directly into the right side of the brain, like drawing water from a well; music, movement and dance; touch and its systems of massage and acupuncture; bio-rhythms and lunar cycles; meditation at the third eye; listening with the inner ear; and mandalas.

The importance of cultivating these modes for cultural as well as individual healing cannot be stressed enough. Our country now relies almost totally for its images on mass media and advertising, both of which play to our lowest common denominator, greed. These images pander to the most superficial aspects of our lives while ignoring the symbols that could really bond us as a human community (and to the rest of nature, the world and the cosmos). A society unconscious of its deeper symbols or unable to create new ones can, as we have seen with the rise of totalitarian systems, easily fall prey to manipulation. You can't ward off burning crosses with Kentucky fried chicken. The development of more rational modes, rather than serving as a defense against this kind of control, merely makes us more vulnerable. Only intuition itself can transform symbols fixed in meaning, stale, inflated, susceptible to corruption, into images that are vital, fresh, expressive of the moment and meaningful enough to raise our consciousness and revitalize our overall perception.

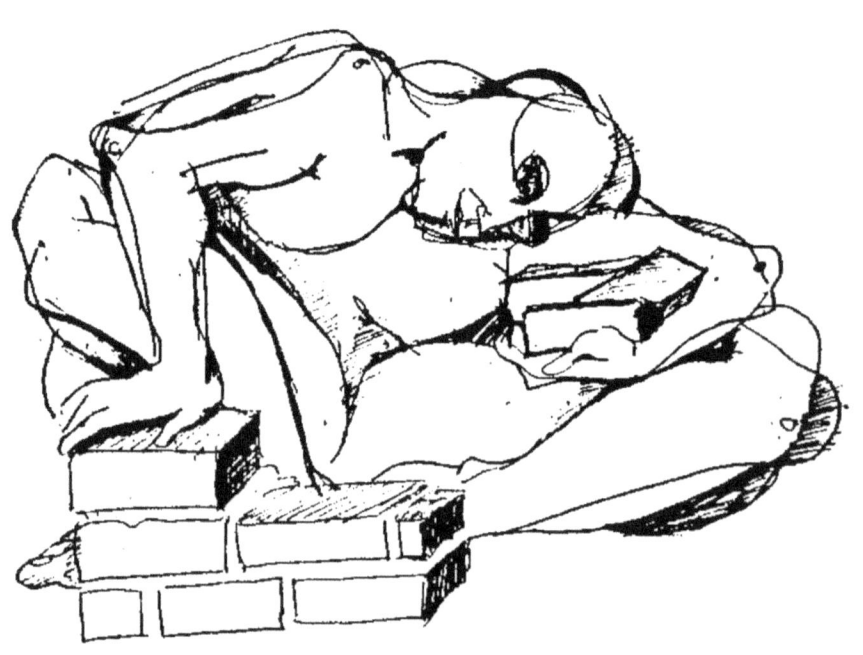

seven

shaping basic units

Sentences and paragraphs are the fundamental units a writer works with, developing skill in their practical formation within a variety of contexts. Like a carpenter, the writer is aware of the traditional uses of these materials, as well as innovative craftsmanship which can adapt set models to special visions and purposes.

Paragraphs, the basic forms a writer builds with, are like walls, filling in the shape of the entire work, sometimes following established blueprints, sometimes not. Structurally each should have its own organizational unity, as well as provide a connection with the paragraphs before and after to form a coherent shape. These links are usually, but not always, provided by transitional expressions which serve as signs to the reader indicating where you've been and where you're going.

While the following paragraph, for example, makes its own contribution by its climactic and ironic structure, it also serves as transition (the initial "but" and the question with which it leaves the reader: Why pigeons?):

> *But the loneliness of the city was brought home to me one early sleepless morning, not by men like me tossing in lonely rooms, not by poverty and degradation, not by old men trying with desperate futility to be out among others in the great roaring hive, but by a single one of those*

> *pigeons which I had seen from my hotel window, looking down at midnight upon the smoking air vents and chimneys.*
>
> —Loren Eisely, "Endure the Night"

The organizational unity of a paragraph usually follows its purpose: analysis, illustration, description, definition, transition, and so on. Although purposes of paragraphs can range widely, one can view their formation in terms of the same functions mentioned earlier—thinking, intuition, sensation, emotion—each organized around a particular focus, a unifying idea, symbol, sensation, or emotion. The beginning writer is encouraged to make this structure clear in a topic sentence. The more advanced writer can bypass this kind of labeling, like the skilled carpenter going beyond the simple box shape, to leave spaces, like windows and doors, between the lines.

The following paragraph, for example, is keenly a unity; it can even be called a comparison paragraph. But the topic sentence, if there is one, is the first four words:

> *Like him was I, those sloping shoulders, this gracelessness. My childhood bends beside me. Too far for me to lay a hand there once or lightly. Mine is far and his secret as our eyes. Secrets, silent, stony wit in the dark palaces of both our hearts: secrets weary of their tyranny: tyrants willing to be dethroned.*
>
> —James Joyce, *Ulysses*

> *All I know about grammar is its infinite power. To shift the structure of a sentence alters the meaning of that sentence, as definitely and inflexibly as the position of a camera alters the meaning of the object photographed.*
>
> —Joan Didion

Sentences provide an even more subtle form of structuring than do paragraphs. Although they contain smaller units of meaning, they themselves are the most basic patterns we can work, with to establish rhythm and emphasis.

As patterns, or overarching curves of meaning, sentences have their own integrity apart from the combined effect of the words and phrases they are made up of. Children utter meaningful vocal patterns or statements before they even know words to fit into them. We can usually tell what a person is trying to say with a sentence even when we don't hear or understand some of the words within it. If you don't believe this, try conversing with someone through jibberish. This form of communication works because certain patterns, certain recognizable rhythms, convey universal attitudes or situations. The rhythm of anger, for instance, is, in almost any language, distinguishable from the rhythm of reverence.

Rhythm is motion based on the patterned recurrence of elements. It is, in sentences, a matter of syntax and meaning, as well as pure sound. Every good writer discovers, after much experiment and exposure to other rhythms, her/his own characteristic rhythm or pulse, just as s/he learns to hear her/his own unique voice. This certain beat underlies all the ways we modify the rhythm of our expression according to different moods, subjects and audiences.

As a writer develops sensitivity to sentence rhythms, certain general kinds are not difficult to isolate:

1. **The colloquial** is characterized by an apparently random flow of language as from a person speaking spontaneously and informally in a conversational tone. Within this there are degrees of intimacy and naturalness. Here John Aubrey writes of Sir Walter Raleigh's execution:

> *He took a pipe of tobacco a little before he went to the scaffold, which some formal persons were scandalized at, but I think 'twas well and properly done, to settle his spirits.* (Brief Lives)

2. **The expository** is characterized by restrained, unemotional style appropriate to rational demonstrations, descriptions, explanations. Devices for heightening rhythm (e.g. alliteration, regular stresses) are used sparingly; parts cohere logically, with a sense of meticulous placement. Expository rhythms move with a quiet poise; do not confuse

them with the inert, graceless sprawl of much information writing, e.g. textbook style. Expository rhythms range from the simple, almost colloquial to the more florid, almost rhetorical:

> But the poet, Aristotle says, never makes any real statements at all, certainly no particular or specific ones. The poet's job is not to tell you what happened, but what happens: not what did take place, but the kind of thing that always does take place. He gives you the typical, recurring, or what Aristotle calls universal event.
>
> —Northrup Frye, *The Educated Imagination*

> Between the unanswerable question and the unquestioning answer we have the rhythm of the work of Poe; at one extreme, an enfolding: the terror of annihilation, the embrace of self and a monomaniacal concern with the preservation of identity, the probing and dissecting of inner reality; at the other extreme, an unfolding: the quest for a personal unified field theory, the searching of the universe for incontrovertible evidence that no soul is greater than his own, the clipping and pasting of a cosmic reality.
>
> —Publication of the Modern Language Association

3. The rhetorical is characterized by an emphatic, insistent rhythm designed to move an audience directly to emotional response:

> This past, the Negro's past, of rope, fire, torture, castration, infanticide, rape; death and humiliation; fear by day and night, fear as deep as the marrow of the bone; doubt that he was worthy of life, since everyone around him denied it; sorrow for his women, for his kinfolk, for his children who needed his protection and whom he could not protect; rage, hatred and murder, hatred for white man so deep that it often turned against him and his own, and made all love, all trust, all joy impossible to achieve—this past, this endless struggle to achieve and reveal and confirm a human identity, human authority, yet contains, for all its horror, something very beautiful.
>
> —James Baldwin

4. **The baroque or stream of consciousness** is characterized by the rhythms of a mind living through the experience. The widest variety is possible, depending on the character whose experience is being created. Often the baroque and the colloquial are indistinguishable since they give the effect of experience seized moment by moment, but the baroque typically conveys a sense of intensity or urgency or profundity, transcending the matter-of-fact:

> *I was crying not to someone, something but (trying to cry) through something, through that force, that furious yet absolutely rocklike and immobile antagonism which had stopped me—that presence, that familiar coffee-colored body...*
>
> —William Faulkner, *Absolom, Absolom*

Another way to use sentence rhythms is for *imitative* effects. Take, for example, this sentence (read it aloud):

> *And when he (the headmaster) leaves the room, lurching rather heavily from side to side and hurls his way through the swing doors, all the masters, lurching rather heavily from side to side, hurl themselves also through the swing doors.*
>
> —Virginia Woolf, *The Waves*

The sentence itself lurches rather heavily from side to side, with its weighty balances: of parallel structure, of word for word repetitions; of rising then falling meters. Although imitations of purely physical motion have a limited usefulness, they can also, as in this passage, suggest psychological and other insights.

A key to imitation, whether physical or psychological, is pacing. Note the different rates of speed in these three passages:

> *Strether hadn't pressed him as to the object of the preference so unexpectedly described; feeling in the presence of it, with one of his irrepressible scruples, a delicacy from which he had in the quest of the quite other article worked himself sufficiently free.*
>
> —Henry James, *The Ambassadors*

In the jolt of my head I heard somebody crying. I thought somebody was screaming. I tried to move but I could not move. I heard the machine guns and rifles firing across the river and all along the river.

—Ernest Hemingway, *A Farewell to Arms*

Below us, men shot downstairs five and six steps at a time, moving in the weird light of flash and flame in long dream-like bounds.

—Ralph Ellison, *Invisible Man*

In the first, James' deliberate, involved and much-qualified sentence echoes the scrupulous caution expressed by his character. In the second, Hemingway's energetic but rigidly contained rhythm suggests both the racing of psychological intensity and the immobility of the situation. In the third, Ellison begins his sentence with a physical rushing, then suddenly decelerates into slow motion.

In addition to establishing rhythm, sentence patterns can be designed for emphasis. Often it is only through revision that a writer can discover the most expressive way of highlighting certain aspects of meaning and casting others into the background. To become more aware of how different structures give different emphases, one often must rewrite the same sentence many times. Although we usually know what is important and what subordinate at the first writing, we don't always clarify this for the reader through the way the sentence is structured.

Sometimes by trying to emphasize too many things at once, a writer will lose the sharper thrust to be gained by focusing on just one element, leaving the reader in a muddle as well. A first step toward clarity is to prune away all the deadwood (wordiness, repetitiousness) in a sentence, and then examine what's left. Often two wobbly sentences can be combined into one forceful one, or one awkward sentence trained into two graceful ones. Sometimes a more satisfying emphasis can be achieved by chopping off dangling endings or beginnings and grafting or burying them in the middle.

The options are limited only by one's imagination and patience, although a certain amount of restraint is recommended when playing with established patterns of syntax. This word of caution is not to discourage innovation or wit but just to warn you that people react to departures from traditional expectation, and calling attention to your style this way should also serve your overall intent.

Shaping the basic units of paragraphs and sentences can often be the most tedious part of a writer's work. Ironically the more successful the job of creating unity, continuity, rhythm and emphasis, the less aware the reader will be of all the effort that went into it. The more such work reinforces meaning, the less obtrusive it will be. A highly skilled style gives the reader a sense of freedom and pleasure in pursuing the experience being described, rather than an appreciation of the writer's cleverness. A well crafted structure supports the reader's interest rather than drawing attention to the writer.

eight
the power of words

A writer, almost by definition is a person enamored with words. This love, like all attachments, can be both a blessing and a curse.

It is a blessing when it leads one to explore the resources of language with respect for its power and integrity. It is a curse when it leads one to overestimate the importance of words—detached from context, community or meaningful activity—and to manipulate them for ulterior purposes, as in rhetoric, propaganda, and grandstanding. Further degeneration of language is signaled by bureaucratic gobbledygook, profession jargon, political deception, and cleverness for its own sake rather than the sake of telling the truth.

To understand the power and integrity of language, we must be in touch with its deepest sources. Recent studies reveal that vibrations felt by the fetus in the womb are expressed by the infant at birth in a complex system of body language accompanied by corresponding sounds which are gradually translated by the child into words and sentences through communication with parents or other caring and responsive adults.

Words are powerful, therefore, to the extent that they are integrally connected to significant relationships, sounds, gestures, actions and vibrations. The transforming power of Sanskrit "mantras" or phrases used in meditation practice testify to the effectiveness of certain sounds and vibrations even when the actual language is foreign to the person using it. President Nixon's "expletives," combined with the gesture of turning off the tape recorder, proved to be far more telling of his contribution to American politics than his formal speeches.

> *The loneliness of the liar / living in the formal network of the lie,/*
> *Twisting the dials to drown the terror / beneath the unsaid word.*
>
> —Adrienne Rich

To avoid the common pitfalls of diction or word choice—trivialization, obscurity, triteness, deception, elitism—writers need, first, to be aware of their own language systems, and second, the languages of those they wish to communicate with. To ignore either pole of this language continuum is to risk non-communication.

One's own language system includes a personal dimension—words, phrases, sounds, gestures that are particularly charged for oneself ("key" words, either positive or negative, which have had a significant impact on one's consciousness)—and a social dimension— words, phrases, sounds, gestures which were dominant expressions in the culture in which one was raised. The more we have cut off these original resources—either 'through cultural shame or societal repression—the less vital our diction will be. Many people would sooner listen to an impassioned speaker in an unknown tongue than a dry speaker whose language is absolutely correct and predictable.

For those who grew up speaking another language or another dialect, the translation into "standard English" will obviously be more laborious than for those who grew up speaking, more or less, standard English. This process of translation, if it does not require one to cut off the flow of one's original language, sensitizes one to the reverberations of words as nothing else can. It can also be painful. When one wants to use an expression for which there is no established equivalent—"Be" in the Black dialect; the feminine universal "She"; *ciao; chutzpah; chi; karma; machismo*—one must risk scorn or stereotyping to introduce it into the vernacular. Of course without these risks having been taken, our common language would be a lot poorer.

When it comes to an awareness of the language of one's audience, ironically, those skilled in the art of translation are probably more advantaged than those who assume that everyone grew up to the academic beat of standard English, since so few in this country actually do. For this reason, and others, people who grew up speaking dialect, if they don't get pitted against each other, have a better chance of communicating with each other than the people who learned only the English we speak in school. In any case, the diversity of our culture requires that *everyone* must reach beyond the words s/he grew up with in order to reach someone else who grew up with a different vocabulary.

Fortunately for all of us, American English, because it has borrowed freely from all the languages which have poured into this country, is rich in words that can refer to the same reality but vary in connotations and sounds. This provides a challenge for writers in picking their way among the countless possibilities. Even so-called standard English, used by educated people in fairly formal communication, is somewhat flexible. Certainly in the general public dialogue, rigid guidelines fall by the wayside regularly, and those who compile the dictionaries which render words acceptable or obsolete are routinely revising their entries.

In the hands of the skilled writer, our common language may range without inappropriateness into a variety of idioms: colloquial, slang, dialect. The surest guide to word choice is not an external stylistic authority but a renewed sense of the experience you want the words to create. In the world of words as in the physical world, it is the inner ear that allows one to keep one's balance.

One test, in fact, of honest diction is to select words which are sayable *for you*, words that you don't feel embarrassed reading aloud. What one writer can utter comfortably, another perhaps cannot (words, as we pointed out in the chapter on *tone*, do create the effect of a person speaking, although they are usually more varied in written diction than in actual spoken use). But this test is not cliché-proof, as it probably will let through whatever trite or vague expressions you are in the habit of using.

An observation on one specific problem with diction: students typically use a higher and higher percentage of adverbs and adjectives as they move through the years of their formal education. This diction, defining and qualifying as it does, may be useful for reflecting a learned approach. However, you may have to take conscious steps *not* to overuse adjectives and adverbs—even in learned writing—since they are more useful in spelling-out than in re-creating.

Choices of vocabulary are reflective of differences of purpose and mood, as well as context, speaker, and audience. An analysis will call forth a more neutral, detached diction than writing that is more impassioned, sensuous, or imaginative. A large, diverse audience of strangers will probably move you to tone down your diction, eliminating words you might use quite spontaneously with a group of friends. Words spoken on common ground paradoxically become fewer and simpler the more that ground expands.

The poet, of all writers, is one who must be most sensitive to the sound, root, charge, shade, tone and connotation of each word. No writer, however, can afford to be unfamiliar with how connotations work. *Resourcefulness*, for example, is a good trait; *cleverness* is good too, but the word suggests superficiality. An *ingenuous* person is straightforward, guileless, but if you call him *naive*, there is a suggestion of simple-mindedness.

Every word has its own weighting, the more so because English has acquired so many words with complicated suggestive power. In general, English words derived from Germanic origins will be concrete, of one or two syllables, down to earth. Words derived from Latin will tend to be abstract and polysyllabic. *Expedite* is Latinate; *hustle, speed* are Germanic, and so too probably is *hurry*. Words adapted from French tend to be less concrete than Germanic words, and often—because they were introduced into England by ruling-class Normans—suggest social organization or polish. Compare, for example, *work* (O. English) with *labor* (Fr.). Compare, for that matter, the suggestions of *association* (Lat.), *society* (Fr.), *club* (O. Norse).

Wherever the words come from, in practice writers are always search-ing for the power of individual words, sifting them to catch sounds, meanings, connotations they want and to exclude those they don't want. Some writers find the dictionary and the thesaurus deadening; others find them invaluable for sensing the freshness, variety, simplic-ity and precision of words. For every writer, weighing and choosing the exact word will be a part of all the other processes of writing, revising and polishing. Although torturous for some, easy for others, the end result will not necessarily indicate which piece of writing was the most labored over.

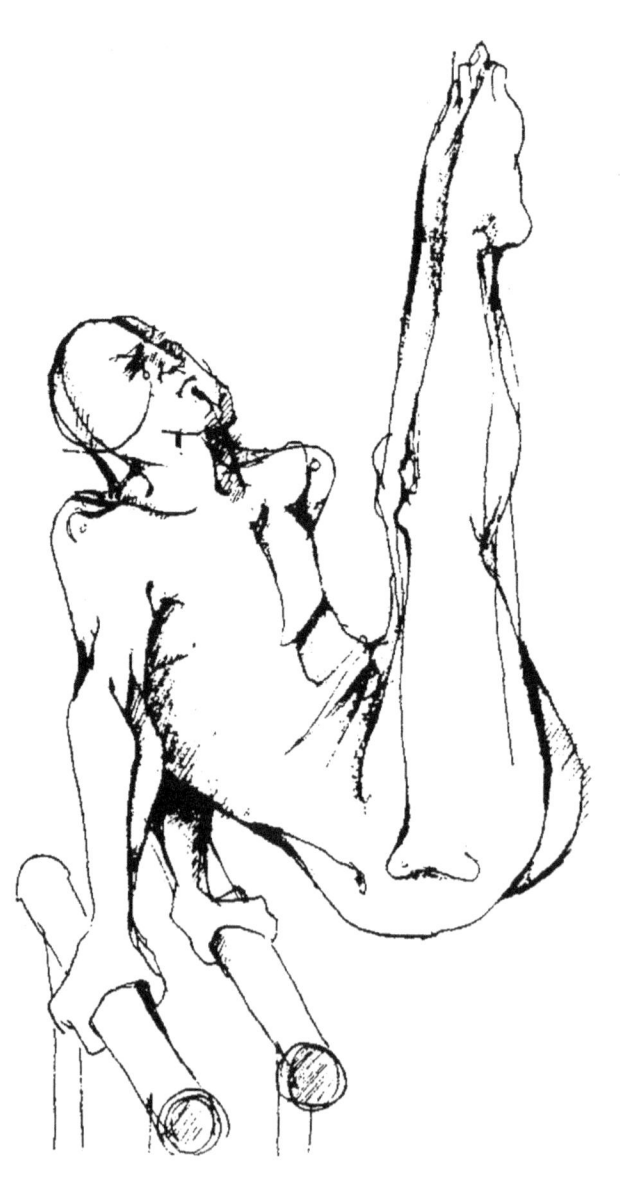

nine

the sustained act of writing

When one seeks to move beyond the first draft and bring a work to completion, a number of questions arise: How do you mold all your resources into one unified, polished piece? How do you allow its own integrity to structure it? How do you sustain reader interest? Given all the available options (tone, perspective, imagery, and so on), how do you bring them together to achieve one overall purpose? How do you know when it's finished?

The simplest approach is to begin at the beginning, don't skip the middle, and follow through to the end, then do it all over again, and again, and again. But of course the process itself is not that simple. What may seem like a beginning at first might shift as you go over the material: Do you want to focus on the beginning of an event? on the beginning of your telling it? or on the beginning of your knowing what the meaning of it is? Each of these would require a different departure point.

To decide finally where to start one must first answer the question: the beginning of what? To discover this answer one often has to go back to the seed of the experience which prompted the initial writing. That seed contains a clue to the overall structure or flowering of the piece. The structure of *a* work is more than just a skeleton or outline. It is the deepest source of perception and integrity, that which holds everything together. One type of organization will reveal a different experience than another. To know which type of organization one should follow, one must remember how the experience was originally perceived. Each mode of perception follows its own line of growth.

The thinking mode has an idea as its principle of organization, often summed up in a thesis statement. It presents an experience along developmental lines of cause and effect, induction or deduction, relying on reasoned analysis. (This is the kind of organization for which the outline or précis is most appropriate.) Structurally it tends to build a box around one idea, to define limits, to allow for orderly progress, and to provide measurable dimensions. For example:

> *One question arises at the very outset. Old age is not a mere statistical fact; it is the prolongation and the last stage of a certain process. What does this process consist of? In other words, what does growing old mean? The notion is bound up with that of change. Yet the life of the fetus, of the new-born babe and of the child is one of continuous change. Must we therefore say, as some have said, that our life is a gradual death? Certainly not. A paradox of this kind disregards the basic truth of life—life is an unstable system in which balance is continually lost and continually recovered: it is inertia that is synonymous with death. Change is the law of life. And it is a particular kind of change that distinguishes aging—an irreversible, unfavorable change; a decline.*
>
> —Simone de Beauvoir, *The Coming of Age*

The intuitive mode has a symbol or metaphoric pattern as its principle of organization, and it presents an experience along exploratory lines which lead to ever expanding connections, relying on poetic leaps. Structurally it tends to trace a spiral around a central image or symbolic design, moving around it with incremental repetition in order to explore all levels of its meaning. For example:

> *We shall not cease from exploration / And the end of all our exploring / Will be to arrive where we started / And know the place for the first time. / Through the unknown, remembered gate / When the last of earth left to discover / Is that which was the beginning; / At the source of the longest river / The voice of the hidden waterfall / And*

the children in the apple-tree / Not known, because not looked for /
But heard, half-heard, in the stillness / Between two waves of the sea.

—T.S. Eliot, *Four Quartets*

The sensitive mode has a sense impression or series of impressions as
its principle of organization. It presents an experience along the lines
of external stimulus and internal response, relying on detailed description. Structurally it tends to cut up one whole impression like a pie
into many parts, so that it can be tasted from every possible angle. For
example:

The grey sea and the long black land; / And the yellow half-moon large
and low; / And the startled little waves that leap / In fiery ringlets
from their sleep, /As I gain the cove with pushing prow / And quench
its speed in the slushy sand. / Then a mile of warm sea-scented beach /
Three fields to cross till a farm appears; / A tap at the pane, the quick
sharp scratch / And blue spurt of a lighted match, / And a voice less
loud, through its joys and fears / Than the two hearts beating each to
each.

— Robert Browning, "Crossing at Midnight"

The emotional mode has an emotion or conflict as its principle of organization. It presents an experience along the lines of tension, climax,
turning points, and resolution, relying on dramatic narration. Structurally it tends to follow an action up one side and down the other like
a mountain trail rising and falling. For example:

Were they angry at me often, or only sometimes? Did my father feel
he'd done well with his life, or that he was a total loss, or did he feel
anything? Did my mother feel pleased when she saw him come in from
the barn, or did she think to herself—or aloud—that she'd married
beneath her? Did she welcome him in bed, or did she make a habit of
turning away and muttering she had a headache? Did he think she was
the best lay he'd ever had or did he grind his teeth in hardly suppressed
resentment at her coldness? No way of knowing. Why should it mat-

ter now, anyway? They remain shadows. Two sepia shadows in an old snapshot, two barely moving shadows in my head, shadows whose few remaining words and acts I have invented. Perhaps I only want their forgiveness for having forgotten them.

—Margaret Laurence, *The Diviners*

Once the structural mode of the experience becomes clear, the writer can begin to trust that an organic structure will unfold out of the work itself. But this does not happen automatically.

Not every seed planted bears fruit. Writers must be willing to respect the integrity of the experience itself enough to listen to what they have written to see if it rings as true as the original. Then, if they can hear the reverberations deeply enough, they must be willing to trim whatever tones, notes and passages, however clever or insightful, do not contribute to the overall pattern of the original. Finally, once this recording is honed down to its essential core, it must be allowed to expand according to its own rhythm and purpose.

Here's where many of us can get lost—in the middle. Having grasped the central import of the piece, we may be impatient to share this with the reader, skipping over the necessary step-by-step unfolding of the process. Like the marathoner who took a subway during the race so she could win without running all the way, or the daredevil who hurls his cycle over chasms to gain an attention harder to capture by less drastic methods, we seek instant gratification and lose that gradual development natural to most processes.

In cultivating the middle there are certain issues of purpose, pace, emphasis, variety, pattern and form that we need to deal with, no matter which mode we are using. In what order should we present the material? How close or detailed do we need to get? how distant or abstract? How fast do we want the piece to move? how slow? How long should each section be? Where, when and how should we vary these factors in order both to emphasize the important points and to maintain reader interest? What final form will it all take?

There are no rules, only options. The creative challenge for any writer is putting all these aspects together to suit her/his own purpose and piece. If a writer has a clear purpose in mind from the outset, selection of options to support this purpose becomes easier. Such a goal—to tell a story, to show or describe something, person or place, to explain, to argue a position, to share a fantasy—can serve as a backbone linking together the disparate parts of the piece.

Purpose, however, while providing direction, is too broad a measure to guide us in mapping out the work for emphasis and pacing. Knowing where we are heading does not, in other words, tell us how to get there or how long to take. To figure this out we need additional options. The following chart shows a variety of methods which range in tempo and immediacy from fast to slow and from concrete to abstract:

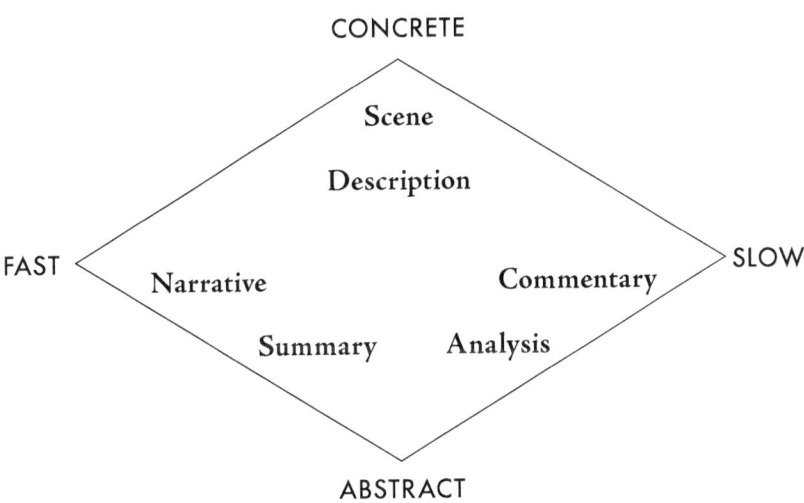

Forester's A *Passage to India* offers samples of each:

> **Summary:** *Houses do fall, people are drowned and left rotting, but the general outline of the town persists, swelling here, shrinking there, like some low but indestructible form of life.*

Narrative: *Now and then she paid tribute to the present, said how friendly and intelligent Aziz was, ate a guava, couldn't eat a fried sweet, practiced her Urdu on the servant.*

Scene: *"Oh, cut the cackle and let's have the verdict," the Major growled.*

Description: *Immediately another flame rises in the depths of the rock and moves toward the surface like an imprisoned spirit.*

Commentary: *Inside its cocoon of work or social obligation the human spirit slumbers for the most part, registering the distinction between pleasure and pain but not nearly as alert as we pretend.*

Analysis: *If she had shown emotion in court, broke down, beat her breast, and invoked the name of God, she would have summoned forth his imagination and generosity.*

Objectively, to intermingle these elements for variety, pacing and emphasis seems simple enough. The real challenge, for which there is no one solution, is to balance them for greater reader interest. It cannot necessarily be assumed that the reader is more interested in the concrete rendering or in the faster tempo. Some scenes of dialogue are as dull as others are intriguing; some analyses are as evocative as others are deadly. Nor can it be assumed that the reader cannot take too much of anything, however good. Many modern novelists, for example, successfully omit summary, analysis and commentary as unjustified intrusions by the author.

One way of sustaining reader interest is to follow—or obviously depart from—a definite pattern of development, one perhaps already proven by writers before us as effective in holding audience attention. These patterns, while not to be identified with the unique structure of the piece, can enhance it because they usually tap into deep designs of perception and revelation in human experience and consciousness.

Some of the most familiar of these patterns follow naturally from the thinking mode: definition, explanation, and illustration; comparison and contrast; movement from cause to effect or from effect to cause (or from one effect becoming the cause of another effect); classification (or a list of kinds or types); step by step process analysis (this last is also useful for the sensitive mode).

Another familiar pattern is the climactic structure natural to the emotional mode: a build-up of suspense, an increase of tempo, a growing tension toward a high point of revelation or a turning point of resolution. From Greek drama to modern detective stories this is the classic structure.

Other tried and true emotional patterns are *ascendency*: overcoming an obstacle or solving a problem; *discovery*: coming to truth out of confusion or blindness; or having a new, unsuspected world open up (as on a journey or visit); *choice*; a significant decision, after moving among two or more possibilities; and *unresolved*: a discovery that leads to the inevitability of further tension or reflection.

But if one wishes a level structure (with hope of climax which never comes or is muted; with no hope; with gradual though never triumphant insight) or an anticlimactic structure, one must turn to other patterns to sustain reader interest.

One useful pattern, especially in the thinking and sensitive modes, is to keep giving the reader new information, new examples, new points. (It is interesting to note that the most effective advertisements have been found to be those that feed the reader a considerable amount of information). This requires that writers know their subject thoroughly and in concrete detail. A supporting variation of this pattern is to acquaint the reader with people to whom the topic is vital and to show where it fits into their lives. If the subject *per se* doesn't sustain interest, the people might.

Another pattern one can use is the balance between unpredictability and inevitability. *Unpredictability*, functional surprise, should dominate the first half of a work, and *inevitability*, functional fate, the second half. This way the seeds planted in the first half should be integrally related to the flowers which bloom in the second. At the level of suspense, curiosity will carry a reader to the point where interest in designs of solution, characterization or plot take over, sparked by the delight most of us feel in spotting clues, guessing, answering questions, then recognizing where they lead. Although this formula can become pat or manipulative, as in certain TV soap operas or situation comedies, it does not preclude significant, even profound, treatment, as in Dostoyevsky's *The Brothers Karamozov*.

Space and time are other familiar ways of patterning a piece. The spatial pattern is often used in the sensitive mode as a way of organizing sense impressions within an immediate environment: for example, perceiving the light from dawn to dusk; feeling stress from top to toe; allowing what is felt inside to register on the outside. On a more expanded scale, the spatial method can help draw a circle for the intuitive mode to operate within: as in a mandala or medicine wheel where the directions (north, south, east, west, center, edge) become symbolic.

Chronology is one of the most common patterns, whether it is used linearly, cyclically, or psychologically. Linearly it often focuses on one event, following its unfolding minute by minute, hour by hour, day by day, year by year. Used cyclically, it focuses upon the pattern of repetition of events, *déjà vu*, history repeating itself, seasons, cosmic cycles, as well as the pattern of transformation: birth, death, rebirth; growth, decay, revolution. Psychologically it focuses on the inner consciousness of events which expand or contract according to their impact on the observer or participant (a duration in which years may pass in a flash, or a moment last for hours).

With chronology a writer is often dealing with subtle interactions of different levels of time. In narration the writer must create the illusion of passing time, both internally and externally: there must seem to be enough time for opinions or characters to change or confirm themselves, yet events must seem to happen rapidly enough to catch characters by surprise. Or a writer may be interweaving descriptions of several events which are occurring simultaneously or in sequence, perhaps on contrasting scales (a nation at war/the birth of a child).

Because chronology must tie in closely with other factors, it can take on many subtle shadings. Did the events happen to the speaker? Or are they told by someone who has heard the story second hand? Have the events just happened or are they recollected sometime later? If so, are they recalled in tranquility or in agitation? A mind obsessed by past events, as Willy Loman's in *Death of a Salesman*, for example, might experience a distorted chronology.

Although on the surface the simplest of patterns, chronology can also be the most complex. In Robert Frost's "The Road Not Taken," for instance, the same event is narrated twice, with rather complicated time shifts. The first telling, apparently not long after the choice of roads, is matter-of-fact and full of qualifying phrases. The roads, we are told, were "really about the same." The second telling comes as the speaker—with ironic humor—foresees himself as an old man looking *back* at his youthful choice. This time, without actually lying he will heighten and oversimplify, making himself a hero. "And I—/ I took the one less travelled by." Note too how the "I" is emphasized.

Finally there is the infinite variety of patterning character revelation, from the seemingly all-inclusive presentation of interiority in stream-of-consciousness to the dramatic rendering of character where the reader is given insight which the person himself is unaware of. Self-centered characters like Ferrara in Browning's "My Last Duchess" and the speaker in Eudora Welty's *Why I Live at The P.O.*, for example, may not see their own pettiness. This pattern of revelation enables the reader to see traits—and possible consequences—that the character himself doesn't know about.

Sometimes, where there is no mystery about the character, as in *Huckleberry Finn*, the pattern follows from the character's own experience. We recognize him basically for who he is and move along with him, seeing events through his eyes. But there is a kind of psychological pattern in which the person leads us, and often himself, toward the revelation of some central but hidden part of his existence. In this kind, of course, emphasis is less on events than on the character himself. The major plot events occur *within* the character. The danger with this pattern lies in holding back revelation, just for surprise effect, and falling into melodrama.

After making decisions about principles of organization, purpose, and pattern, a writer needs to choose a form for the work. It is important that your finished piece not sound like a writing assignment. Any form your heart desires will probably serve, if you're willing to work at it, but some might obviously suit your purpose better than others. Some options are: a letter, a newspaper column, a magazine article, a short story, an excerpt from a novel, a biography, a speech, a poem, a play, a scientific description, a nature book, travel book, children's book, health book, artist manual, how to organize pamphlet, an organizational skit, or a backyard musical.

The form you choose is, like the pattern you follow, not to be confused with the actual structure of the work, which will have its own unique integrity. Writers who try to structure their work according to established formulas often fall into the conventional and the clichéd. If we compare the work to a living creation, then purpose provides backbone, pattern shows characteristic movements, and form is like skin, fur, feather, or clothing— that which makes the piece accessible and recognizable to the audience. Structure is all this and more; it is the actual integrity of the piece.

Finally, having explored all these options, you are ready to go back to your beginning and know the piece for the first time. To the reader it should seem that the rest of the story or article grows out of the first paragraph, but for the writer it is equally true to say that the first paragraph grows out of what follows. And in *fact,* the best openings are often written *after* the main part of the story or article is done. By then the author is more familiar with the themes and characters and has a surer judgment about what to show first.

To sustain reader interest you need to be sure to win interest at the start. The first paragraph should say what you want to say, start spinning the world you want to show, catch the reader up into absorbing lives and issues. It should disclose enough to intrigue the reader and to lead him toward later revelations.

Be careful though. There is a lot of rather mechanical lore about first paragraphs—they should be enticing, exciting, action-filled, function as a "hook." All these things are true at the right place and time, and you should practice until you are confident that you can achieve them. But over-devotion to them can lead to strained or gimmicky openings.

A good test of your openings—and sometimes a remedy for bad ones—is simply to remove the first two or three paragraphs. Were they essential? Writers at some time or other delay the real opening of a story or article while clearing their throats. A brisk pace is often helpful—yet the following initial paragraph of a novel, although leisurely, manages to make an impact, to get the reader directly involved in what is happening, and to raise more questions than it answers:

> *The assassination of President Olivero, which took place in the autumn of 1861, was for the world at large one of those innumerable incidents of a violent nature which characterize the politics of the South American continent. For twenty-four hours it loomed large in the headlines of the newspapers: but beyond an intimation, the next day, that General Iturbide has formed a provisional government with the full approval of the military party, the event had no further reverberations in the outer world. President Olivero, who had arranged his own assassination, made his way in a leisurely fashion to Europe. On the way he allowed his beard to grow.*
>
> —Herbert Read, *The Green Child*

If you have the right beginning, you should be able, structurally, to follow it through to the end, whether bitter, sweet, bittersweet, or artificial (does anything ever really end?). Then you'll find yourself returning again to your beginning to go over it all again— rewriting, cutting, pasting, expanding, contracting, reordering, patterning. Last but not least, when you've run out of patience, excitement or energy, when there seem to be no new insights to glean from going over it, you know that it's finished—for the time being. Some pieces are never finished; some, like this book, get "done" years after they were written.

other books by Margaret Blanchard

NONFICTION

The Rest of the Deer: An Intuitive Study of Intuition

Restoring the Orchard: A Guide to Learning Intuition (with S.B. Sowbel)

Duet: A Book of Poems and Paintings (with S.B. Sowbel)

From the Listening Place: Languages of Intuition

NOVELS

Hatching

Wandering Potatoes

Who?

Queen Bea

Change of Course: the Education of Jessie Adamson

This Land (a novel memoir)

Where? An Allegorical Novel

Water Spies

about the author

S.B. SOWBEL

Margaret Blanchard has lived in central Vermont for many years—after adventures in the city of Baltimore, then sharing land in the Adirondack woods. She's now retired in Montpelier. A writer, stained glass artist, and educator, she has published books on intuition and creativity as well as poetry and a variety of fictions. She has been active in movements for civil rights, peace, women's rights, gay rights, as well as union, community and environmental organizing. Retired from teaching in the M.A. program of Vermont College, she is currently engaged in Northern Lights, the *Bridge*, Courage & Renewal, Unitarian Universalist Sunday School and Social Responsibility, and Creativity Circles.

She found these maps and guides helpful and hopes that you do too.